DR PETER GR[
nationally reco[
adaptive resilience, stress, and performance.
He is a founder and managing director of
London Integrated Health Ltd. and Adaptive Resilience Ltd. He is also a co-founder and Chief Medical Officer of RCube Health, a digital health start-up company that has developed a mobile app for stress management and resilience (RCube).

Peter works as an Honorary Clinical Specialist in Sleep Medicine and General Medicine for the University College London Hospital (Royal London Hospital for Integrated Medicine) and in private practice (London). He is an Associate Fellow at Said Business School, Oxford University, where he conducts Adaptive Leadership Resilience workshops for senior civil servants and major project leaders of the Cabinet Office. He also provides workshops and trainings for senior civil servants and lawyers at the United Nations.

Over many years he has practised meditation and has followed the spiritual and highly practical methodology of anthroposophy and *The Philosophy of Freedom* as founded by Rudolf Steiner. Peter is a member of the Anthroposophical Society and the Anthroposophic Medical Association and the Christian Community, and is the author of the *The Quiet Heart: Putting Stress into Its Place* (Floris Books 2007) and *Manifesting your Best Future Self* (Building Adaptive Resilience, 2020).

His website is: www.mastering-life.com

MASTERING LIFE

*Rosicrucian and Magical Techniques
for Achieving Your Life's Goals*

Dr Peter Gruenewald, MD

CLAIRVIEW

Clairview Books Ltd.,
Russet, Sandy Lane,
West Hoathly,
W. Sussex RH19 4QQ

www.clairviewbooks.com

Published by Clairview Books 2022

A CIP catalogue record for this book is available from the British Library

ISBN 978 1 912992 42 3

Cover by Morgan Creative
Typeset by Symbiosys Technologies, Visakhapatnam, India
Images on pp. 28 & 43 by Mina Gajovic
Printed and bound by 4Edge Ltd, Essex

A Note to the Reader

Acknowledgements

My special thanks go to my publisher and editor Sevak Gulbekian, and to Tom Ravetz and Angus Jenkinson, without whom this book could not have become what it is now. They have refined it with practical advice and encouragement.

I am also grateful to my wife, Bereke Dzhantelieva, whose patience, support and understanding has majorly contributed to the completion of this book.

Contents

Foreword

The poet John Keats described life as the 'vale of soul-making'. He articulated the all-too-real difficulties that confront individual aspirations along the course of life. It is these Dr Peter Gruenewald addresses. He is a medical doctor, who also specializes in physiological and mental coherence. Coherence allows healthy self-regulation while also providing the inner ground for an effective life, even in difficult circumstances. Despite – or perhaps because of – the plethora of technological aids to contemporary living, modern civilization has not eliminated stress. It is arguably increasing. Despite better opportunities emerging for some marginalized groups, finding a fruitful path to the realization of one's own potential is far from straightforward. Very many people feel unfulfilled!

Therefore, I am glad to encourage the reading and use of this book. It is a guide to an inner practice, one that can make a significant difference to how life unfolds and to what purpose. Dr Gruenewald explains how the cultivation of self-mastery, learning to realize one's own highest potential, may make a positive difference not only for oneself but also for others. Beyond the selfish self is the resourceful self that has much to give. Peter outlines a simple, yet richly organized, meditative practice originally inspired by the polymath philosopher, Rudolf Steiner. The approach, based on freely forming and focusing on inner symbolic content, is akin to others such as ethical individualism, mindfulness, Buddhism, Christian contemplation, even the contemporary practice of many elite sporting celebrities, who build inner pictures to achieve goals.

Peter succinctly but carefully guides the reader on this valuable way of self-mastery in the face of the crises in nature, society, and in the situations of very many. It encourages inner truthfulness as a counterforce to fake personality. It stimulates coherence with the needs of others; love and care for the needs of the Earth. It bolsters attainment of good goals.

In this respect, a short note on the reference to Christ within the text may be helpful. As Peter outlines it, this refers not to the image cultivated in various religious denominations, but instead to what might be called the universal Logos, a sublime principle of creativity and love that belongs in every heart and is needed in every situation. This universality is evidenced by the fact that the core of the meditative practice stems from Egyptian civilization. It is modified for modern humanity, but it testifies to the timeless search of the individual to know themselves, and in doing so know the world in all its wonder. What is then discovered will astonish.

Angus Jenkinson
Moreton-in-Marsh, Cotswolds, May 2022

Preface

Using magical symbols for the achievement of goals and success is not only empowering but also fraught with risks. It should therefore be practised with caution. A magical mastery of life needs to go hand in hand with mastery over oneself as well, including personal moral development. Exerting power without enlightened moral development can easily lead to an abyss of abuse and destruction. However, these risks should not hold us back from seeking to master ourselves and life, in close connection with those spirits that serve the ascendance of humanity.

This book is a guide that helps identify our life goals in harmony with the goals of the ascending evolution of humanity – the development of inner freedom and selfless love. These harmonic goals are supported by the spiritual world, serving the development of everyone. They are enhanced by the meditative use of magical symbols and mantras. In this inner work, we can call upon the assistance of spiritual beings and masters, including members of the hierarchies of angels that serve the ascending development of humanity towards inner freedom and love. As we will see, one of these masters is Christian Rosenkreuz, whose contemporary Western, Christian path of initiation has influenced civilization in often unrecognized ways. For many years, his pupils have used Christian magical symbols and mantras for meditative and ritualistic work. As we will also see later in this work, the methods for the practice of Christian magic given in this book are closely connected with the

'Temple Legend' of Hiram and Solomon. This legend was important to high degree freemasonry as well as Rudolf Steiner's Esoteric School.

This book is a practical guide that introduces a comprehensive and effective training to better meet our spiritual and personal developmental needs, including the needs of family, friends, society, humanity and nature. A spiritual symbol and a mantra for meditation are introduced that can enhance our personal and spiritual development and speed up our capacity to manifest our harmonic goals through strong action and the attraction of favourable outer circumstances.

Combining goal contemplation, visualization and symbol and mantra meditation can lead towards the development of – and control over – spiritual forces and skills. These work within us, in nature and in our destiny.

Using contemplation (courageous conversation with our resourceful self), meditation and spiritual symbols to enhance imagination and willpower, in order to ask spiritual beings and their forces to assist in goal achievement, is a path of practical magic.

To harmonize one's own goals with the developmental needs of other people and humanity (harmonic goals) is an important process to safeguard against the abuse of occult power. Use of occult power for purely selfish means or to harm others is a path of black magic that ultimately guides us away from the developmental goals of inner freedom and love, and into the abyss of dependency to dark occult powers. The path described here, on the other hand, intends to strengthen the development of wisdom, beauty and goodness within ourselves and others. Unfortunately, any gain in power can also be abused for dark purposes.

The meditative practice and the process of goal realization are supported by resilience-building techniques,
active listening, mindful nature observation and the contemplative work with the initiatory Temple Legend. In
many ways, these techniques are an important preparation
for actual meditative work, as they strengthen selflessness,
love, imagination and the capacity to focus our mind and
growing willpower.

Introduction

Have you ever experienced that, despite your best intentions, you lack the strength to manifest your life goals into reality? Do you feel the pain of not being able to bridge the gap between your ideas, ideals and your everyday life? Have you been confronted with inner and outer powerlessness due to being unable to develop the inner discipline and outer strength required to see your goals through to their realization? Have you asked yourself how to become more effective in helping yourself and other people? If these questions live within you, with the burning desire to transform yourself and the world around you – inspired by the will to help yourself, others and humanity – then this book is for you.

My sense of disempowerment and my inability to bridge the gap between my ideals and goals and my life's reality led me to embark on the path of anthroposophy and Rosicrucian white magic. It led me to write this book, sharing my insights and experiences on the path to the being of Christ and towards a life of empowerment and alignment with my true self. It also helped in my work as an integrated physician, anthroposophic doctor and resilience and leadership coach.

Christ

The Christ referred to here is not bound to any religious denomination or confession. Since his birth, life on earth, death and resurrection, Christ manifests within us as selfless love. When we consciously and purposefully relate to our higher self – the Christ consciousness within us – Christ's beneficial influence reaches into the inmost part of our being.

Christ is the 'I am that I am' (in his appearance to Moses in the burning bush); the 'Not I, but Christ in me' (in St Paul's description); and the 'I am the Alpha and Omega' (as described in the Revelation of St John).

Asking Christ – the Sun Spirit, co-creator of the world and source of cosmic love – through our daily symbol and mantra meditation to reside and work within our head and heart, can over time enlighten our thinking to become free, our feeling to be filled with selfless love, and our will to be magically empowered to act in accordance with the goals of human evolution.

I have used the approach outlined in this book in my life for many years, and have found it very helpful to reach my goals and ideals over time; to live with the discomfort created by the discrepancy between those goals and my current reality; and, ultimately, to realize those goals in my life. This approach helped me to develop patience and deal more effectively with inevitable setbacks and inner and outer resistance, and to acquire new skills on this path.

I have also introduced many elements outlined in this work to my clients in my resilience workshops. Most of the techniques described here, such as 'coherence breathing', mindful nature observation, courageous conversation with yourself, visualizing techniques, gratitude practice, etc. have been scientifically validated in terms of their benefits for emotional health and wellbeing and their impact on human relationships. They have proved to be very helpful for the personal, spiritual and overall development and wellbeing of my clients.

This book is a guide to assist you in your personal and spiritual development and goal achievement. It supports the manifestation of individual, communal and global goals through highly developed imagination, aligned with empowered will. Meditative use of spiritual symbols and mantras can train and enhance the power of our imagination and the power of our will to the point where we can transform our intentions into reality more speedily and comprehensively. This should be done in an ethical and holistic way, avoiding binding others into dependency (achieving power over others for the sake of exploitation and personal gains) as this may lead ultimately to an entrapment in materialism. Instead, personal, communal and global goal manifestation work should aim to extend egotism beyond its boundaries and transform it into altruism. This can be achieved through widening our self-interest and fully embracing increasingly larger circles of influence – from family, friends and colleagues, to community, country, continent, humanity, the earth and universe. I will from now on call those personal goals that are aligned with the developmental needs of individuals and humanity, *harmonic goals*.

Connecting our harmonic goals with a distinct spiritual symbol and mantra can help develop skills that instrumentalize spiritual forces, allowing one – more speedily and comprehensively – to manifest goals to advance our own as well as others' development. Harmonic goals can concern anything from personal and spiritual development to personal, social and communal health and wealth; personal and professional success; to charitable goals that compassionately address the ills and misfortunes of others, assisting the general development of humanity. To be harmonic, our goals must serve the spiritual development of the individual, of groups and of humanity as a whole in our development towards freedom and love, truth, beauty and goodness.

Of course, none of our goals should conflict with the integrity and personal and developmental needs of others. It requires a careful process of selection to assure that our goals do not only support our own development towards self-determination (freedom) and love, but also the development of others, in the sense I have described above.

If occult symbols and mantras are misused for selfish gain or to harm others, this opens a path of black magic that ultimately leads away from what is truly human. Through regular contemplative (goal exploration), meditative (goal individualization) and decisive action (goal realization), augmented by spiritual symbols and mantras, our goals can increasingly become refined and aligned with the developmental goals of humanity. In this process, we can extend our egotism and gradually and effectively embrace the needs of others.

*

Spiritual symbols are images of hidden spiritual processes, conditions and forces that relate to spiritual beings such as elementary beings, hierarchies of angels or even the being of Christ. When we connect with these symbols through meditation, we effectively open ourselves and merge with those spiritual forces associated with these spiritual beings. Ultimately, we learn to master these forces in collaboration with those spiritual beings, first within and then around us.

The forces behind these symbols and mantras must be applied in such a way that we realize them within us during the meditation – that we absorb them into our being. Spiritual symbols and mantras are suitable meditation objects that, through sufficient practice, can open the soul to its own spiritual perceptions – but also to the willful mastery of those forces that are represented, helping us to manifest our true and loving intentions more speedily and in effective collaboration with others.

It is important that the symbols and mantras are so easily manageable that their complete structure can be spanned by one's waking consciousness at any time. It is also important to contemplate the meaning of these symbols and mantras prior to using them in meditation. We need to understand them fully, to feel and love their meaning, and to want to connect with the spiritual reality they relate to, purposefully and willfully. This should be a continuous process, making the symbols more alive and impactful within our meditation.

The meaning of the symbols and mantras, i.e., the spiritual reality to which they refer, are also multidimensional and ultimately inexhaustible, and their meaning and power can only gradually be revealed and mastered by our knowledge and will through continuous meditation. If we wish to, we can aspire to manifest truth, beauty and goodness within our professional work, allowing it to support the development of our fellow human beings and humanity towards extended consciousness and empowerment, and ultimately towards freedom and love.

On the other hand, spiritual techniques can also intentionally exploit others, brainwashing them through social media and the internet, for example by flooding people with too much information, fake news and tempting imaginations that they lose the capacity to discriminate between truth and lies, love and hatred, goodness and evil.

We can be governed by doubt (as we become unable to trust our own judgement to explore the truth); hatred (racism, misogyny and xenophobia) and fear; coming to accept a totalitarian world order that trades personal freedom and liberties for seeming safety and security. The motivation for this trade-off may often come from a place where we try to manage our fears by giving up control, exerting excessive power over others, or both. The outer tools for this development can be politics and economics, amplified sometimes by corrupted science. Some people may use these spiritual and psychological techniques to enslave human consciousness. Selfishness can become a dominating force in the lives of those who strive for power without moral compass and benevolence.

In contrast, we may align our life's purpose and goals with the ascending forces of humanity. We should be ambitious, striving to achieve our goals, gaining power and influence – but this power and influence should be inspired by wisdom, goodness and beauty, serving the development of love and freedom. These are the core harmonic goals we should aspire to when using symbol and mantra meditation to manifest for practical, magical purposes.

Power without wisdom and love turns into violence; wisdom without love and power turns into intellectualism; love without wisdom and power turns into deluded fanaticism.

*

Let's now look at the symbols that will be introduced in this book, beginning with the Tau cross and Sun.

The Tau cross is an ancient symbol that played a major role in the practice of spiritual mastery in Atlantis (Tao), in Egypt (ankh) and during the building of the Solomonic temple through Hiram Abif (Hiram's hammer). It is built from two parts: a vertical and a horizontal bar. The lower, vertical bar stands for the principle of power, and the horizontal bar for the principle of love.

In the Temple Legend (see Chapter 11), master builder Hiram receives wisdom from Solomon for the building of the Solomonic temple. Hiram has the love, power and craftsmanship to build the temple and thereby brings Solomon's ideas and plans into physical existence. With the help of the mythical Tau cross (hammer) he collects the workmen around him to complete the building of the temple and uses the hammer to complete the creation of the brazen sea, a symbol for the harmony of fire (power) and water (wisdom).

In the Egyptian ankh – the Tau cross with a loop (see Chapter 12) – the loop represents the developed pineal gland, the so-called 'third eye', the eye of Horus – a spiritual organ that is localized behind the point between the eyebrows, in the centre of the brain. The Egyptian mysteries defined the ankh as the 'key of life', and meditating on the Tau or ankh can train us to master the forces of life within and around us. The Tau cross as a spiritual symbol represents the development of freedom, love and success.

Imagining in our meditation the Tau cross below and the sun in our pineal gland and heart, calls up for the forces that help us to develop freedom, love and power over ourselves, as well as the power to achieve (gain mastery over) our individual goals, in harmony with the goal of the ascending development of humanity and earth (harmonic goals). In the Temple Legend, Hiram receives the golden hammer (Tau cross) and the golden triangle, in order to aid the development of humanity. His initiation into freedom, love and mastery enables Hiram to return as Christian Rosenkreuz, the leading spiritual master and teacher within Western Christian spirituality.

Christian Rosenkreuz

Christian Rosenkreuz (1378–1484) is the legendary founder of Rosicrucian initiation and the worldwide esoteric brotherhood, the Rosicrucians. According to Rudolf Steiner, Rosenkreuz is one of the highest Christian initiates and spiritual masters, leading the development of humanity towards an understanding of the Christ impulse and the development of Christ consciousness. He works as one of the great leaders of humanity, bringing true 'heart knowledge'. As we will see later, he is the author of the Temple Legend, the *Fama Fraternitatis* (1614) and the *Confessio Fraternitatis* (1615).

The Tau can be used as a meditation symbol that can help manifest our goals faster than would happen under normal conditions, allowing for acceleration of spiritual and personal development. We will give practical instructions as to how to widen egotism into altruism and to learn to co-create, effectively and speedily, our individual future and the future of others. This is done by aligning our thoughts, feelings and intentions with the symbols and mantras of this meditation.

As a preparation for this process, we should work on self-mastery in daily life by practising self-exploration and

self-improvement, as well as active listening and mindful observation of nature. The techniques described here
can help to profoundly strengthen our 'I' (or higher self)
and to develop our ability to align and harmonize thinking, feeling and will. They can also enhance our power
of imagination and the strength of our will, contributing
to a purification of our inner self and the development of
enlightenment and love. The mental and spiritual training
given through these techniques, and the contemplation of
symbols and life goals, should always be practised along-
side regular meditation in order to avoid complications.

Practising the 'Mastery of Life' meditation (given
below) may also help on the path of personal and societal
development towards a healthy balance between individualism and collectivism based on freedom (self-determination) and love, and ultimately prepares for the creation
of new communities based on selfless love. Anyone who
believes that we can be responsible co-creators of our destiny may also live with many burning questions, such as
the following:

- Are self-determination and co-creation of our destiny a reality or simply a delusion?
- Can we effectively become co-creators of our destiny, and how can we do so?
- How can we prevent ourselves from abusing power?
- How can we make sure that our goals do not cause
  harm to others – which could lead to failure or
  disaster?
- How can the realization of my life goals become
  an act of genuine creation, therefore becoming part
  of my development towards truth, beauty and
  goodness – rather than a projection of my past and
  present self?

- How can we align our goals with the deeper needs of our family, work colleagues, friends, neighbours, communities, country, world community, humanity and nature?
- How can we make sure that the manifestation of our goals will not intentionally or unintentionally damage ourselves, our loved ones, our neighbours, competitors, friends and enemies, to an extent that is unacceptable to us and others?
- How can we learn to contribute actively and effectively to build a brighter future for ourselves, our communities, nature and humanity, whilst fulfilling our self-defined needs?

Becoming increasingly capable of changing the trajectory of our own and other people's lives as well as the life of our planet, comes with the obligation to extend our sense of responsibility, ethical values, awareness – our love and desire beyond ourselves – in order to let our growing insights, our care, love, compassion and deeds serve an ever-growing circle of people. In this process, we may embrace not just our needs and those close to us, but also increasingly the needs of groups, of humanity and even the life of our planet. Growing power without growing personal and global responsibility may lead to corruption – and ultimately to destruction. The saying 'Be careful what you wish for' has an even deeper meaning, considering the growth in willpower that we can experience through inner techniques (NLP, hypnosis) and outer science-based technology.

Here are some examples of challenges we are confronted with:

- We live with the knowledge that the world's nuclear weapons could destroy the planet.

- We are aware of growing economic and social inequality, based on the greed of a few, that could destroy the fabric of our society.
- We are in the process of destroying the earth through global warming, intoxification of land, air, rivers and seas, with enormous consequences – such as flooding and the reduction of biodiversity.
- Industrial farming may contribute towards an increasing risk of viral infections, passing from animals to humans, possibly preparing the ground for further pandemics.
- Digital technologies could replace direct human interactions (screen time, social networks, computer games) from earliest childhood onwards, with significant negative consequences for the development of the consciousness of the child, their social skills, and physical, emotional and mental health.
- Principles of collaboration and social responsibility are being replaced by Darwinist principles of adaptation, ruthless competition and the philosophy of 'the survival of the fittest'.
- Fake news has sometimes replaced striving for compassionate truth.
- Democracies are at risk of being replaced by populist authoritarian regimes.
- Fierce battles are being fought for resources, such as drinking water, food and fossil fuels.

From this backdrop, let us revisit the statement 'Be careful what you wish for'. As individual and collective selfishness and egotism have a potentially destructive effect on society, humanity and our planet, the resulting question may become: *How can we apply the process of co-creation in an ethical and sustainable way, that serves humanity and our*

deeper intentions for benevolence towards ourselves and others,
and doesn't ultimately cause harm and destruction?

First, we can learn and practise daily to extend our conscious awareness, our compassion and our deep interest and benevolence beyond ourselves and our loved ones, including ultimately our whole planet. This will allow us gradually to transform selfishness into altruism. This is not so much about the overcoming of our ego, but about our ego becoming sufficiently broad that it embraces passionately the needs of the whole world, responding in a knowledgeable, authentic, truthful, compassionate and benevolent manner.

As we move away from a 'me' perspective to an 'us' approach, we experience a widening of our consciousness and conscience that over time can become more global and inclusive, without losing touch with our family, friends, community as well as our daily tasks and work. Including others within our goal setting, affirmations, visualization and meditation can help us to grow in our capacity to transcend our ego and connect with our true self as well as the true selves of others. Contemplating our goals in a courageous inner conversation with ourselves – by sincerely exploring what impact they have on our loved ones, communities and the world at large – can help us carefully to select our goals before committing to them. This exploration is not only retrospective or rooted in the past; it is also a prospective and creative process. It allows us to invent, design, pursue and create our own life and that of humanity.

This contemplation, or courageous conversation with ourselves, not only allows us to explore what we want to achieve, it also makes us aware of why we want to achieve our goals, and how achieving them will impact on others – what inner and outer obstacles we may face

in implementing these goals, and how we might mitigate identified risks and obstacles through collaboration
and concrete action.

Such a prospective and truly socially-inclusive thinking
is not purely abstract; it is an ethically creative process that
involves our higher feelings, such as passion, compassion,
enthusiasm, love and gratitude, as well as our goodwill to
serve our true self and others. This contemplation, practised regularly, can fundamentally change the trajectory of
our lives and the life of our planet. It is a skill which we
as individuals must acquire for the sake of future genera-
tions. This is not just a process that can be applied by us as
individuals; it is quite plausible that a charitable group of
people can decide to apply these techniques collectively,
for their community or humanity as a whole.

Connecting the results of this contemplation process –
our life goals – with an understanding of the central role
that Christ plays for the future evolution of humanity, can
take the process of co-creating our destiny in conjunction
with the destinies of others, including humanity and the
earth, to the highest level.

Contemplating the deeper meaning of these symbols
allows us not only to understand them, but also to love
them and the spiritual forces and beings that are connected
to them. Connecting with the forces behind symbols and
mantras – as we work towards manifesting our ever more
altruistic goals – is a continuing spiritual-physical path
towards developing freedom and love, and supporting the
creation of communities that serve the ascending evolution
of humanity towards freedom and love.

As we identify, love and pursue our own deeper developmental needs, in conjunction with love for the needs of
other individuals, humanity and the planet, we experience

that this unfolding love will in the future contribute towards an abundance in our and other people's lives.

Personal selfishness and social-Darwinist practice have created a world of exploitation, contrasting unimaginable wealth with heart-breaking poverty, and wars with profound suffering and destruction. In contrast, it is necessary that an increasing number of people wake up to this suffering and sow the seeds for future societies to be built on social justice, love, truth, beauty and goodness, and also the facilitation of human development and the redemption of nature. This may be achieved through self-knowledge and inner development, and by communally pursuing ideas, ideals and visions of social justice, the overcoming of poverty, preserving and renewing nature, etc.

I believe that no political manifesto of any kind will be capable of bringing sustainable changes about. Rather, the creation of open and transparent communities founded on spirituality, truth, freedom and love, can achieve the necessary changes. Just like the thoughts and visons that were for example fostered and prepared in secret societies decades prior to the actual social events that led to the French Revolution and the American constitution, meditative and ceremonial work with the spiritual forces that underlie the ascending development of humanity will lead us out of this period of darkness and destruction and into the light and warmth of new societies built on free and loving individuals and communities.

It has been the intention of Rudolf Steiner and Christian Rosenkreuz, as well as other spiritual masters and teachers, to contribute towards this development. But it lies in the inner freedom of each human being as to whether or not they wish purposefully to connect with these initiates in order to serve Christ and the development of humanity in love and freedom.

Rudolf Steiner

Rudolf Steiner (1861–1925) was a spiritual scientist and teacher who was initiated by Christian Rosenk- reuz. He renewed the Rosicrucian teachings, making them accessible for contemporary human conscious- ness. Steiner's philosophical and scientific training, combined with his highly developed clairvoyance, allowed him to develop a practical esoteric path of training that not only inspires and renews many pro- fessional activities, but also helps people find their personal path of development. At the heart of Steiner's work stands his individual relationship with Christ and Christ consciousness, enabling community build- ing that is built on the foundations of freedom and selfless love.

Humanity's thoughts, ideas and beliefs of the past have contributed towards the development of practical materialism, ruthless competition and the exploitation of humans and nature on a grand scale. On the other hand, many people have fallen prey to fanatical nationalism and ungrounded and unworldly Eastern spirituality, or a mixture of unworldly spirituality and materialistic impris- onment. The modern Rosicrucian path is one of balance between these extremes: transforming matter into spirit through wisdom (science), beauty (art) and power (eco- nomics, politics and technology). It simultaneously brings spiritual ideas, beings and forces into existence, changing the world through our inspired will.

Fostering thoughts and ideas built on a truly holistic, spiritual-physical understanding of the human being and a deeper understanding of the history of developing consciousness and the potential future development of humanity, can lay the foundation for a brighter, socially-just, and abundant future – abundant for everyone.

The Mastery of Life meditation introduced in this book connects us with Christ within and around us, in order to achieve our goals in alignment with the developmental goals of humanity. Spiritual symbols and mantras are focal points and true conductors of powerful spiritual forces that can accelerate our development and enhance the positive and healing influences we can have on our destiny, the destiny of others and the destiny of our planet.

In our goal contemplation – courageous conversation with ourselves – our questions regarding our life goals may grow deeper and wider over time, including our heartfelt and genuine sense of responsibility. Then, our goals and the motivations of our actions will lead us to results that are born out of love, and that can contribute towards the betterment and survival of humanity and earth.

Altruism is not just about others; it also includes our own personal and developmental needs. Otherwise, it may turn into sectarianism, burnout and co-dependency. Altruism is not a process of self-denial; rather – as we have seen – it is a process of widening our egotism and increasingly making it all-inclusive. An abundant life ultimately means abundance for everyone – and it would not be true abundance if the abundance of the universe could not potentially be accessed by everyone!

The process of contemplation helps us to explore our goals in a socially-inclusive and responsible way, and to extend them to others. We then embrace these goals with love and passion and turn them from abstract thoughts into inspiring ideals. Through creative visualization, we impregnate the subconscious part of our will with our freely chosen and created ideals, so that they turn into motives for action. We reorganize our will, so that implementing our intentions becomes natural and seamless. We then connect with other individuals, society and nature in a non-judgemental, loving, compassionate way, by exploring their needs selflessly whilst suspending judgement.

By aligning our goals with Christ, we align our goals with the life-goals of others, embracing all levels of need and development: physical, emotional, mental, spiritual and social. The creative powers of the world and destiny then meet us halfway, by allowing the circumstances that enable us to manifest our ideals and visions into a new reality.

To summarize the steps of this process:

1. We explore our goals and the conscious motivations of our actions, identify them and embrace them with love and enthusiasm.
2. We apply the technique of creative visualization, imagining how we want to conduct ourselves in order to achieve our goals, and picture what it feels like when we have achieved them – picturing the future as if it is happening now.
3. We develop a concrete strategy to mitigate risks and overcome obstacles.
4. We commit to the actions required to implement our goals.
5. We explore the world around us with an open heart, mind and will in order selflessly to perceive and embrace the developmental needs of these aspects of ourselves.

6. We conceptually, emotionally and intentionally link our goal to the Mastery of Life meditation, in order to align it with divine will.
7. We contemplate the meaning of the symbols and connect with their spiritual reality through our feelings (love and enthusiasm) and our will.
8. We practise the Mastery of Life meditation daily.
9. We act upon our newly created ideals, strategies and visions and await for the world to meet us halfway.

During our goal exploration we should consider the developmental needs of others. Thus, manifestation can become an integrated part of self-actualization, leading us to thoughts, feelings, intentions and actions that are sustainable, truly responsible, highly effective and impactful.

In the following chapters, we will describe a practical path towards spiritual development and effective, harmonic goal selection and goal manifestation.

1.
Sun, Tau Cross and
'I am the Alpha and the Omega'

Summary: *This chapter describes the meaning of spiritual symbols and why they are used as symbols in the Mastery of Life meditation.*

Symbols are representations of spiritual processes, conditions and forces. When we connect with them through meditation, we transfer these spiritual forces to ourselves and learn to master them. The symbols must be used in such a way that we *realize them within us* during the meditation – that we absorb them into our being.

Symbols are suitable meditation objects that, through sufficient practice, can open the soul to its own spiritual perceptions – but also to the mastery of the forces that are represented by them. It is important that the symbol is easily manageable, so that its complete structure can be spanned by one's waking consciousness at any time. The meaning of the symbol – i.e. the spiritual reality to which it refers – is, however, multidimensional and ultimately inexhaustible, and its power can only gradually be revealed and mastered by our will through continued meditation.

Why We Use Symbols in Meditation

When using symbols in meditation, we are calling on the spiritual beings and/or forces behind them to be present within our meditative work and within our lives. If these symbols are true, they give us power to develop new faculties that, with continued practice, give us control over these forces. Meditation with such symbols and mantras helps us manage and align the conscious and unconscious creative forces within us, but also the forces between humans and within nature – thus extending the influence of these forces beyond the period of meditation and into our daily lives.

A symbol should be understood through thinking before being meditated upon, and should be charged with our love and intention. It then has the power to incubate our will and to lead us to act according to the forces and meanings it represents, but also invites the spiritual forces in the world to meet us halfway.

When initially concentrating and meditating upon a distinct spiritual symbol, we may experience an inner pain that arises from the fact that we are distant from truly, deeply understanding and communicating with the forces or beings that relate to this symbol. This suffering turns into joy when the true meaning of the symbol is revealed over time, and we can connect with and become increasingly inspired by the beings and forces during meditation and within daily life.

Initially, the imagined symbol may be faint and blurred, but with practice it can appear bright and sharp in one's mind. Although it takes effect whilst it is still experienced in its faint and blurred state, the effect increases with the intensity of feelings and will that focus on the symbol. To enhance the intensity of one's emotions and willpower whilst focusing on the symbol during meditation, you can build up its personal significance for yourself during symbol contemplation (see Chapter 2).

To enhance the brightness and sharpness of the image, you can practise your imagination skills through mindful nature observation (see Chapter 9). In addition, it may also be helpful to imagine in your mind's eye the Tau cross with Sun (see below) in three dimensional form, from all perspectives. During symbol contemplation, the Tau cross with Sun is imagined as if it stands in front of us and then alternates within certain parts of our body (brain and heart). This is done to aid the process and purification of consciousness (thoughts, emotions and intentions), life and body, and to help us master these forces within ourselves and nature.

The Tau symbol used in our meditation is ancient in its origins, and its multiple meanings have been renewed for contemporary human consciousness. It needs to be understood, loved and its meaning intended, so that it can have its full desired effect. We can charge it and make it more effective – both inside and outside of our meditation – by having an inner conversation (contemplation) within ourselves over its meaning for us and for the world. In this process, we connect with it on a cognitive, feeling and intentional level, building an ever-growing relationship with the beings and forces behind the symbol.

Once we meditate on the Tau cross with Sun, we place it in the centre of our awareness and 'rest' within it – imagining and feeling with intention the effect of the symbol and the corresponding forces and beings behind it. At the end of the symbol meditation, we empty our consciousness from the meditative content, stay receptive and remain focused on the activity of meditation, without focusing on the symbol's content, the mantra or our breathing.

Through rhythmic repetition of this meditative activity over time, the magic symbol will not only reveal its true meanings on different levels, but will also help us to develop and control the forces within us, in social life and in nature. It becomes a true tool of human spiritual

development and empowers us in our quest of self-actualization and service for others.

So if, for example, a symbol is the expression of a harmo-
nious alignment of thinking, feeling and will, then strong
meditation upon that symbol puts us on the path to con-
trolling thinking, feeling and will and developing the full
alignment expressed within the symbol. Therefore, just
like a mantra, the symbol becomes an accelerator of human
spiritual, soul and physical development.

The Sun

The sun sends light, warmth and life towards the earth and
the planetary system. On a spiritual level, light is wisdom,
warmth is love, and life is power.

The spiritual Sun symbolizes the Logos, the Son of
God, Christ, who descended from the cosmos into the Sun
Sphere, and from there into Jesus during the baptism in
Jordan, completely merging with him in the final three
years of Jesus' life.

During the Mystery of Golgotha (the crucifixion), the
blood of Jesus Christ streamed into the earth, and the
Christ's Sun aura merged with the aura of the earth. These
earthly sun forces of Christ can also be found within our
heart and third eye when we focus on the Christ Sun
within us, in our heads and also our hearts. The Christ Sun
ultimately helps us to develop the forces that master life
within and around us.

Meditating on the spiritual Christ Sun forces unfolding
within head and heart, allows us to support the development of freedom, love and mastery. Meditating on the spiritual Christ Sun and Tau cross can also contribute towards
the spiritual Christ Sun shining into our understanding of

the world and our actions, lifting them into the realm of sacredness as a service to humanity.

Tau Cross (Seal of Hiram) with Sun

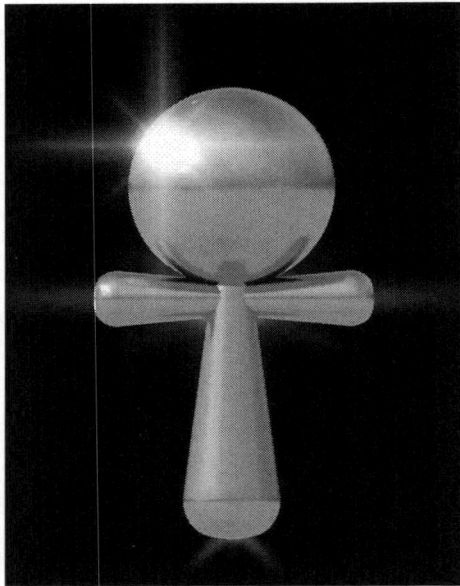

The golden Tau cross with Sun is a symbol of freedom (sun), love (horizontal bar) and mastery of life (vertical bar). The sun represents the purified thinking (wisdom), the horizontal bar represents the purified human feeling (love), and the vertical bar represents the purified will (mastery).

When the Tau cross and Sun are combined in this way, they form the image of a key – a key that can lead to the mastery of life. The Tau cross with Sun symbolizes the harmony of and mastery over thinking, feeling and will, and ultimately over the forces of life within and around us. It stands for the mastery over the all-weaving power of the Divine Tao (vril, prana, chi), of which humanity still had extensive knowledge and influence on ancient Atlantis and Egypt (ankh – the Key of Life). When the Tau cross is thus complemented with the Sun, it represents the development of the forces of the third eye and the heart, and is also a key for the mastery of life.

The Tau cross is the Christian seal of St Francis of Assisi. For Francis, the Tau cross is the symbol of the crucifixion of Christ Jesus, the ultimate surrender of the Logos, the Son of God, Creator of the World, who lived in a human body and suffered death for the salvation of humanity. That the creator of the world became a human and went through the experience of physical death is God's sacrifice, for the salvation of every human being and for humanity as whole. Thus, the Tau cross with Sun is a symbol of the death and resurrection that can lead to the birth of our true self, the 'I am', as well as mastery of life.

I am the Alpha and Omega

In Taoism, the tao is an invisible life force which permeates all realms of creation. This mysterious universal force was acknowledged, honoured and respected as the Tao of Atlantis, and the mastery over this universal life force was symbolized in Ancient Egypt as the symbol of ankh, and in Christian Rosenkreuz's Temple Legend as the hammer.

'I am the Alpha and the Omega' is an esoteric name for Christ. 'I am' is the source of selfless love (in the present); Alpha represents the wisdom of all that has been created (in the past); and Omega stands for the power that will create the future, allowing us to reach our full human potential.

This 'I am' within us learns to master the universal life force. Christ consciousness is ultimately accompanied by the mastery of life within and around us. Connecting willfully with the Christ impulse and the life forces of Christ through symbol and mantra can lead to the empowerment of the 'I am' within, and ultimately to mastery of life.

'I am the Alpha and the Omega' (or 'I-A-O', Iota, Alpha, Omega) is a Rosicrucian metamorphosis of the 'T-A-O', the sound that stands for the universal life force and its mastery through the 'I am'.

2.
Mastery of Life Meditation

Summary: This chapter introduces the Mastery of Life meditation – a practice that combines coherence breathing, symbol contemplation, symbol visualization and mantric affirmation in order to align thinking, feeling and will in head and heart, and to assist the development of spiritual faculties and the achievement of harmonic goals.

Meditation

1. Coherence breathing

- Sit comfortably and upright.
- Preferably, close your eyes.
- Breathe deeply and slowly through your nose, in and out. Fill your lungs with air, from the bottom up. Feel how, at the start of the inhalation, your abdomen expands and how it gently contracts with each exhalation. Once this breathing pattern has been established, focus on your lower, middle and upper back. Feel the resistance of the back of your seat when your lungs expand. Ultimately, you want your lungs to expand to the front and back, filling your lungs like a barrel from the bottom up (barrel breathing).
- Breathe equally long for both your inhalation and your exhalation.
- Gradually, over several days to weeks, slow down the pace of your breathing to approximately six seconds for your inhalation and six seconds for

your exhalation (roughly ten breathing cycles per
minute).

- Do not force the slowing down of your breathing.
  Rather, develop the slow pace gradually, as your
  breathing should always feel comfortable and
  never forced.
- Do not leave a gap between inhalation and exhalation and/or between exhalation and inhalation.
- Initially, fill your lungs with air to only 75%, in
  order to avoid hyperventilation. After a few days
  or weeks of practice, you can try to fill your lungs
  completely (as by then the pace of your breathing will have slowed down sufficiently to avoid
  hyperventilation).
- The unforced slowing down of pace and depth of
  breath during this exercise is a natural result of an
  increasing level of relaxation and focus.
- Should you feel uncomfortable or dizzy, stop
  and take a break and then start over again – this
  time breathing either less deeply or slightly more
  slowly.
- Continue with coherence breathing throughout the
  contemplation and meditation.
- You may require a little practice of coherence
  breathing before moving on to add the next elements of contemplation and meditation.
- After a while, you will focus on the content of the
  meditation and contemplation, and coherence
  breathing will continue without you being aware
  of it.

2. Symbol contemplation

Visualize a golden Tau cross with Sun in your mind.
Describe it in your mind as you view it. Look at it from all
sides, i.e. imagine it as a three-dimensional image.

Now, explore the meaning of the Tau cross with Sun in your mind, using your inner voice and involving your thinking, feeling and will. You may for example contemplate the following:

- The Tau cross with Sun is a symbol of freedom, love and mastery of life.
- The vertical arm of the Tau cross stands for the full empowerment of magic will.
- The horizontal arm of the Tau cross stands for selfless love.
- The Sun symbolizes enlightened thinking, filled with wisdom.
- The Tau cross with Sun together form the image of a key – a key that can lead to the mastery of life and help to manifest harmonic goals.
- It will help me to manifest wisdom, beauty and goodness within my life, and to strengthen my development towards ever-growing freedom, love and mastery of life.
- It connects me with Christ, the Logos. The Tau cross is the symbol for the crucifixion of Christ Jesus, his sacrificial surrender to death; and the rising Sun is the symbol of his resurrection. The creator of the world became human and went through the experience of physical death. Through his death and resurrection, Christ has brought salvation for every human, and for humanity as whole.
- May the meditation of the Tau cross with Sun, as a symbol of Christ's death and resurrection, lead me to the birth of my true self, the 'I am' – the Christ within me – and to mastery of life.
- With the help of the Tau cross with Sun, I call on Christ to help manifest my harmonic goals for the betterment of my life and also other people's lives, and for the development of humanity and earth.

Whilst thinking these or similar thoughts, we should keep imagining the golden Tau cross with Sun in front of our (closed) eyes and generate love and enthusiasm and the strong will to connect with Christ, in order to manifest our harmonic goals through enlightened understanding of the sacredness of nature and social life and through our sacred actions.

A formula given by Christian Rosenkreuz can help us to connect our will and actions, emotions and feelings and our thinking and perceptions with the Divine Trinity, as follows:

> *Ex Deo Nascimur (From God we are born)* – symbolized by the vertical arm of the Tau cross.
> *In Christo Morimur (In Christ we die)* – symbolized by the horizontal arm of the Tau cross.
> *Per Spiritum Sanctum Reviviscimus (In the Holy Spirit we are reborn)* – symbolized by the Sun.

During your contemplation, penetrate your thoughts with feelings of enthusiasm, courage, love and devotion, and also with strong will and confidence, in order to contribute towards the positive development of your loved ones, colleagues, humanity, cosmos and the earth.

This symbol contemplation should take between 5 and 10 minutes.*

3. Symbol Visualization

With each inhalation, focus on your heart, filling it with sunlight, warmth and life, imagining the Tau cross with Sun inside it.

With each exhalation, focus on the centre of the head, behind the point between your eyebrows, and project

---

*To support the contemplation of the above, you can refer to the following lectures by Rudolf Steiner: 'The Royal Art in a New Form' from *The Temple Legend* (Lecture 20), *The Etherization of Blood*.

sunlight, warmth and life into the pituitary and pineal gland area, imagining the sun-filled third eye residing on top of the virtual tau cross.

The two horizontal arms of the cross reach into the left and right brain, connecting both. The horizontal bar lies inside your brain, at the height of your eyes, and the vertical bar follows the direction towards your spine.

4. Mantric affirmation

As you silently speak the words below, feel the connection with Christ. Appreciatively and lovingly, embrace the words below.

As you inhale, imagine the Tau cross with Sun inside your heart and silently speak, feel and will the mantra:

I am the Alpha and the Omega.

As you exhale, focus on the Tau cross with Sun inside your head and silently speak, feel and will the mantra:

I am the Alpha and the Omega.

This part of the meditation, with coherence breathing, imagining the Tau cross and silently sounding the mantra, may take between 10 and 15 minutes.

5. Silent Awareness

Now try to eliminate all images and thoughts, feelings, sensations and intentions. Focus on breathing, and try to maintain an awake, empty consciousness for a few moments. Over time, this may extend to a few minutes. If you get distracted by thoughts or images, perceptions or sensations, focus on your breathing, and then once again empty your consciousness. This will allow you to be touched and inspired by Christ. Spend approximately five minutes in receptive silence.

Ending the meditation

Always follow this meditation with a deep sense of gratitude. You may end with quiet and deep feeling, saying the
following words:

> Thank you, Christ, source of all abundance in my
> life, for helping me to acknowledge the sacredness
> of social life and the life of nature, and to co-create
> the fulfilment and manifestation of my deepest vir-
> tues and harmonic goals through sacred actions.
> Thank you for assisting me in my earthly and spir-
> itual development. May my virtues, harmonic goals
> and achievements always be in harmony with your
> intentions and for the good of everyone.

Contemplation (outside of your meditation)

Contemplate the following outside of your meditative
time:

- Your relationship to Christ, the Trinity and/or
  Christian Rosenkreuz;
- Christ's death and resurrection and its meaning
  for you and for humanity as a whole;
- the meaning of the Tau cross with Sun (symbol
  contemplation);
- the meaning of the mantra 'I am the Alpha and the
  Omega';
- the importance of the development of the third eye
  and heart;
- the importance of the development of freedom,
  love and mastery of life;
- the importance of building communities founded
  on truthfulness and selfless love;

- your personal and transpersonal harmonic goals (including those of your loved ones, your community and humanity).

During your contemplation, penetrate your thoughts with feelings of enthusiasm, courage, love and devotion. Also, with the strong will and confidence to contribute towards the positive development of your loved ones, colleagues, humanity, earth and cosmos.

Conclusion

Meditating the Tau with Sun in conjunction with the mantra 'I am the Alpha and the Omega' can help us master forces of life within us and in nature, and helps us to co-create with the source of creation within us (our higher self) and within the world (the higher self of the earth). On this path, we heighten our capacity for freedom and deepen our capacity to love. We learn to harmonize both activities, so that they complement each other. Based on these qualities, we will shape new communities that support the development of societies that facilitate the ascending evolution of individuals and of humanity as a whole.

3.
Difficulties that can arise during Contemplation and Meditation

Summary: This chapter helps identify difficulties and advises how to overcome them.

In your practice, you may experience one or more of the following problems:

- Distraction by rising thoughts, feelings, images and/or memories.
- Unpleasant emotions and unusual sensations.
- Loss of focus.
- Feelings of dizziness.
- Discomfort around your heart or mild palpitations.

Below, we will address these.

Distraction by rising thoughts, feelings, images and/or memories:

Don't worry about these distractions – your exercise will still be effective. Take an interest in the contents of what arises, then send them away and refocus on your breathing, the feelings and intentions that are associated with the mantras, and your visualization of light and warmth.

Unpleasant emotions and unusual sensations:

Some disturbing emotions can also arise – such as fear and anxiety – which may have been previously suppressed. Memory images or imaginative pictures can surface due to the relaxation process. You may feel sensations of floating and physical weightlessness, increased circulation (warmth), or pins and needles. These feelings are usually mild and transient. They indicate that you need to proceed very slowly, gradually adapting to the new psychological and physical experiences. Temporarily shorten the duration of your meditation and its intensity until you have become adapted. These experiences will stop when the exercise ends. Focusing on your breathing process and the content of your meditation can help to overcome these disturbing emotions and sensations.

Loss of focus:

Don't worry! With practice, you'll find that your capacity to concentrate and focus on the meditation content increases. The training is still effective if you continue with the coherence breathing, even if you're being distracted. Take a brief interest in the distracting thoughts or images; ask them what they want to tell you, then send them away, refocusing first on your breathing and then on the meditative content.

Feeling dizzy:

If you notice any dizziness as you practise the breathing technique, try to breathe less deeply, which should stop any signs of hyperventilation. If you want or need to, take a break. Don't force anything and only practise in a way that feels natural to you. Perform these exercises gently and don't put yourself under any pressure.

Discomfort around your heart or mild palpitations:

This is usually temporary and should soon stop. It's often a sign of psycho-physical release. But if such symptoms persists, you should stop and seek advice from your health professional.

Caution: *Palpitations with a heartbeat that is too slow or too fast, or irregular heartbeat combined with dizziness, chest pain or shortness of breath, are signs of a medical emergency and require immediate attention! This condition can develop entirely independently of the training, but in rare cases may coincide with it.*

Some Tips

Be patient
As you practise this exercise, it helps to remain focused and present. Over time, you'll become increasingly skilled at maintaining and deepening your focus and relaxation. Be patient with yourself and try to avoid being too goal-oriented. Right away, you'll feel great relief from stress and from the effects of negative emotions, but the impact of deep-seated problems on your health and performance may take some time to improve or be resolved.

Build up your mantra and the meditation symbol
Regularly contemplating on the meaning of the Tau cross with Sun and its elements, as well as the 'I am the Alpha and the Omega' mantra, outside of actual meditation will deepen the work and make the meditation and the symbol more effective. Contemplating our relationship with Christ and Christian Rosenkreuz, in conjunction with the symbol and mantra, can help us deepen our relationship with both and access their beneficial influence in daily life.

Set limits
Don't practise the meditation for more than 15 minutes at a time. Practising it for around 15 minutes at the same time every night and/or morning may be most beneficial.

Proceed slowly

During your breathing meditation, you may at first experience uncomfortable sensations, such as mild dizziness. This often is a sign that your own perception of your body is changing or coming into sharper focus. In order to regain control and ease the sensations, take things slowly and open your eyes during meditation. Most of these sensations are short-lived and tend to disappear entirely with practice.

Body position

Initially, it is good to do the meditation in a sitting position, so that you won't fall asleep. But you can also do it standing or lying down, depending on your alertness at any moment and what feels right for you. The aim is to achieve a state of awareness between focus and relaxation where you remain in control of your consciousness.

Your eyes

You may keep your eyes open or closed during the exercise – whichever feels better and more appropriate. Closing your eyes enhances relaxation, whilst opening them enhances alertness. Ultimately, the aim is to remain alert and relaxed with eyes closed, but that may take a little time and practice to achieve.

Dealing with stressful events

As you begin to practise every morning and evening, you'll find it easier to establish a state of focused relaxation at will – before, during and after challenging events in your day. By focusing on, slowing and deepening your breathing, you can change the way you respond to challenging situations within a few seconds. You will feel calmer, more

flexible and creative when responding to challenging situations. This will lead to lower stress levels and sharper
performance when the going gets tough.

Enjoy!
Make practising these exercises enjoyable. This is time with
and for yourself, and it will benefit your spiritual development, health, work and private life, and bring mastery
over life.

Establish a balance between alertness and relaxation
Coherence breathing is not primarily a relaxation technique. It is a powerful balancing exercise that enhances
focus and relaxation. It is at once both calming and energizing. It calms and relaxes you when you are tense and
agitated, and stimulates and energizes you when you are
feeling tired and exhausted. Both sympathetic and para-
sympathetic* activity are enhanced simultaneously.

Distracting thoughts, feelings and images
When you get distracted by thoughts, feelings and images
during meditation and contemplation, do not try to suppress them. Rather, examine them by asking what they are
trying to tell you, and then send them away and refocus.
If this doesn't work, then focus for a few minutes on the
image of a golden rod with a black and white snake crossing at its centre (the Mercury staff or Caduceus). This meditation symbol can help to free your consciousness from
disturbing thoughts, feelings or images and can be practised before meditation or contemplation.

---

*Relating to the part of the autonomic nervous system which balances
the action of the sympathetic nerves.

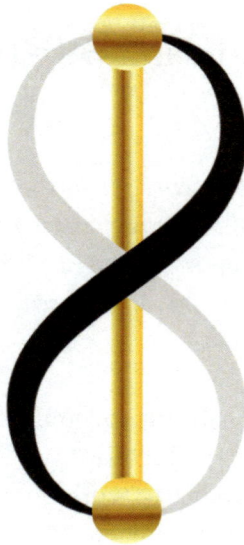

Mercury staff or Caduceus

4.
Self-Exploration and Self-Transformation

Summary: Here we discusse how to explore our weaknesses and shortcomings, transforming them into strengths and skills in order to help develop self-mastery. This is a precondition for deepening our capacity for inner freedom, love and harmonic goal achievement.

Self-exploration and self-improvement are an important part of harmonic self and goal realization. Identifying our short-comings gives us a chance to work on them and to transform potential weaknesses into new inner and outer skills.

Self-mastery is an important step towards mastery of life. Once we have honestly and courageously identified our flaws, we can contemplate how to transform them. Formulating smart and harmonic goals – regarding new skills and personality traits we want to acquire – we can create affirmations, contemplate and meditate on them, and eventually realize them through visualization and enlightened actions.

Self-exploration

Questions to ask:

- What kind of personality traits would I like to transform? Which vices do I want to overcome? Which virtues do I want to acquire?
- Which behaviours do I want to change, and which new behaviours do I want to adopt?

- What kinds of new skills do I want to commit to acquire?
- How can I effectively serve the needs of my family, friends, colleagues, community, nature, earth and cosmos?
- What are the concrete actions I will commit to in order to implement and manifest my true self?
- How do I create an abundant life for myself, for others, for humanity and for our planet?

Steps to take:

- Once you have established your (initial) developmental goal, contemplate how achieving it will impact positively on your life and on the lives of others, as well as on humanity as a whole.
- During contemplation, develop love, enthusiasm and courage for your goal, as well as the confidence that you will achieve it over time.
- Ask Christ to help you with this process of transformation.
- Condense your goal into a simple, positively formulated affirmation in the present tense. For example, if you want to acquire the capacity to develop equanimity in challenging situations, condense it into something like the following: 'I am calm and content, even under pressure.'
- Silently repeat the affirmation with coherence breathing as part of the harmonic goal achievement process. (See further in Chapter 6.)
- Picture yourself living your new personality trait, even within challenging circumstances.

Six Core Skills for Harmonic Goal Realization

The six harmonic goals given below support the development of the brow and heart chakras as spiritual organs for inner freedom, selfless love and goal achievement. They safely advance our development and safeguard against the dangers of self-deceit, selfishness and abuse of power – as well as protecting us from the influence of negative spiritual beings and forces.

It is advised to work on these qualities for one month at a time, and then to begin working on the next one. Maintain the sequence as outlined here. Once you have gone through all the skills (after six months), start again with the first one.

During daily life, we should try to implement these qualities, which over time need to become habits in order to build our character. Do not neglect these qualities and new habits, as they protect from the potentially negative influences of meditative and magical practice, and guarantee a more successful manifestation of your harmonic goals.

Here are the six core skills:

1. **Self-exploration:** How well can I maintain clear thinking, good judgement and decision-making under pressure?
   Goal: *Dispassionate thinking and understanding in all situations of life.*

2. **Self-exploration:** How strong-willed and persistent am I in turning my intentions into actions, even when I experience inner and outer obstacles?
   Goal: *Strong will and persistence.*

3. **Self-exploration:** Can I maintain inner calmness and emotional equilibrium under pressure?
   Goal: *Inner calmness and equanimity.*

4. **Self-exploration:** Am I able to balance negative experiences with positive thoughts and feelings in all life situations?

   Goal: *Maintaining positive thoughts and feelings when exposed to challenging situations.*

5. **Self-exploration:** Am I non-judgemental, open-minded, open-hearted and with open will?

   Goal: *Being able to suspend judgement unconditionally.*

6. **Self-exploration:** Am I able to maintain balance and alignment between my cognition, feelings/emotions and will?

   Goal: *Aligning and balancing cognition, feelings/emotions and will.*

In your contemplation, connect your goal with the following master mantra: 'I am the Alpha and the Omega.'

5.
Creative Goal Exploration

Summary: This chapter introduces creative goal exploration through contemplation (courageous inner conversation) and mental rehearsal (moral imagination). This involves creating ideals as drivers of our actions, and identifying, planning and visualizing the action and achievement of our harmonic goals. Once our goals are aligned with the source of creation within us and within nature, life circumstances may meet us halfway as golden opportunities to realize our harmonic goals.

Contemplation is 'heart thinking' that penetrates our thoughts with feelings, passion and intentions. Contemplation is like an inner conversation with myself, in which I explore the meaning of my thoughts, values and core skills, my relationship with them and the impact that they may have on me, on others and on humanity.

As I contemplate, I strongly commit to my intentions, thoughts, core values and core skills, in order to make them a part of my personality in everyday life. As I contemplate my harmonic goals and core skills, they become full of meaning and power. Contemplation has an energizing effect and charges goals and affirmations, making them more effective.

Start the process by making a list. Formulate questions about an important goal you would like to achieve. You can begin by picking one of the three topics given below. (Of course, you can also create your own questions and replace these with ones that are more appropriate to your own life.)

Topic 1: Abundant Life exploration

- What do physical, emotional, spiritual and social abundance mean for me?
- What do abundant life, abundant health, abundant wealth, abundant business and career success, abundant happiness, abundance in my relationships, spiritual abundance (purpose of life), abundance in my self-development, all mean – in a concrete sense – for me and my loved ones, for my colleagues, community, the earth and universe?
- What does abundant life mean for others, for nature and humanity?
- Which aspect of my abundant life would I like to work on right now?
- How would success and achievement in this chosen area impact on myself and others?
- What are the obstacles and risks involved in becoming successful in these chosen areas of life?
- What are the strategies and what are the harmonic goals and actions I commit to in order to mitigate risks, overcome obstacles and achieve my/our goal/s?
- Visualize performing your actions, mitigating risks, overcoming obstacles and achieving your harmonic goals.
- How will you know that you have achieved your goal? What does it look and feel like?

Topic 2: Symbol exploration

Increase the intensity and effectiveness of your meditation by regularly contemplating the meaning of the symbols of Sun and Tau cross (see Chapter 1).

- Explore the meaning of these symbols in a silent conversation with yourself, engaging not only your thought processes, but also your feelings and your will.

- You can also look at the image of the Tau cross with Sun or just imagine it whilst contemplating the meaning of its different elements and the symbol as a whole.
- When contemplating the saying 'I am the Alpha and the Omega', the esoteric name of Christ (see Chapter 1), ponder with gratitude and devotion your personal relationship with Christ.

Topic 3: Goal exploration

Choose a goal that might be related to an issue with a personal relationship, a work-related goal, career progression or a material possession. Or, choose a goal that concerns the needs of others, nature or humanity. Or, choose another personal development goal.

The Process

Explore the following questions, first in writing and then in a courageous conversation with yourself:

1. Exploration in writing

Work through the following questions:

- What goal would I like to achieve?
- How will achieving this goal impact on me, on others, on nature and humanity?
- What are the inner and outer obstacles I must overcome?
- What risks do I need to mitigate?
- What are the concrete actions I commit to in order to overcome my inner and outer obstacles?

- Visualize for a moment how you implement these actions and what it feels like to do so.
- How will I know that I have achieved my goal? What does it look like? How does it feel?

2. Courageous conversation with yourself

- Once you have worked through questions in writing, put your work aside.
- Choose one or two key aspects of achieving your personal, community or humanitarian goal and have a quiet, inner and courageous conversation with yourself.
- Now, empty your consciousness and create an inner space of focused alertness by concentrating on your breathing only (coherence breathing).
- Next, imagine having an inner conversation with Christ and/or Christian Rosenkreuz. Address them personally, as you imagine their presence.
- Explore your harmonic goal and all questions associated with these goals in a silent inner conversation with these entities.
- Focus not only on your thoughts, but also on your feelings and your intentions. Feel your passion, compassion, joy and enthusiasm, and experience the strength of your intentions and will as you explore your goal.
- Once this conversation is completed, ask Christ and/or Christian Rosenkreuz to assist you in implementing and achieving your goals, thanking them for their assistance.
- Visualize implementing your actions and living your desired goal. What does it look like? How does it feel?
- Finally, connect your harmonic goal with your master affirmation, 'I am the Alpha and the Omega'. This master affirmation will represent your harmonic goal during meditation.

Contemplation allows you to develop feelings of true appreciation and gratitude for what 'abundant life' and achieving your harmonic goals mean for you, your life, your loved ones, humanity, earth and the cosmos. It also allows you to align your thoughts, feelings and intentions around your harmonic goal and to make it truly your own.

As you contemplate abundant life, your harmonic goals and their relevance for you and the world, you will over time penetrate your harmonic goals and virtues with strong feelings and intentions, moving forwards towards manifesting them in your day-to-day life and in your spiritual development. And your newly created destiny will meet you halfway!

Admittedly, the inner conversation with Christ and/ or Christian Rosenkreuz may be difficult at first. You may feel that you get distracted and lose focus – initially, your thoughts may wonder off, inner doubt may arise, and your heart and will may not be completely in it. When you are distracted, just refocus. If you need to do so initially, keep your eyes open in order to maintain control of your thoughts. As with any new process, you will need some practice to develop mastery. With a little time, you may progress quickly on your path. Be patient with yourself initially and embrace any progress you make with gratitude.

Once you have completed this process of harmonic goal exploration and connected that harmonic goal with your master affirmation, you will be ready to connect it with the magic symbol of the Tau cross with Sun, and to enhance your capacity to manifest your harmonic goal in life through enlightened actions and the support of Christ and Christian Rosenkreuz. (See also Chapter 6.)

6.
Harmonic Goal Manifestation: Empowering the Will

Summary: *This chapter introduces a meditative and practical technique to enhance goal realization, with coherence breathing, symbol, mantra and inspired actions.*

Once you have identified, contemplated and visualized your goal (see Chapters 5 and 6), you can do the following to enhance your goal realization:

Preparing harmonic goal manifestation through contemplation

- Contemplate your life goal/s and the abundant life you wish to create.
- Connect your harmonic goal through contemplation with the master affirmation. For example, say to yourself: 'These harmonic goals are represented through the Tau cross with Sun and the master mantra, I am the Alpha and the Omega'.

Mediate your goal affirmation

Practise coherence breathing and maintain it throughout the meditation.

Confirm silently that you commit to co-create your goals in collaboration with Christ and/or Christian Rosenkreuz, and ask them for support in implementing your harmonic goal.

Project the Tau cross with Sun into your heart with each inhalation, and into your head with each exhalation.

Silently repeat your master affirmation, 'I am the Alpha and the Omega', with each inhalation and with each exhalation – thinking, feeling and willing it.

Know that your inspired and empowered thoughts, feelings and actions will help to bring these harmonic goals into manifestation, and that the world will meet you halfway in the process of your goal manifestation.

Be patient:
It takes time to deepen your meditation, to empower the symbols and mantras, and to transform the inner and outer resistance you may experience in manifesting your harmonic goals.

7.
Transforming Negative Emotions

Summary: Here we examine how we can effectively deal with pressure and negative stress in day-to-day situations, and to transform negative stress and extreme emotions into a source of spiritual and personal development.

Context: Negative emotions are not negative *per se*; they fulfil an important function in our life. For example, anxiety and fear can make us more cautious, whilst anger can lead us to confront injustice, etc. Negative emotions are truly negative when they are fixed and experienced at the wrong place and time. Then, they lead to tension or paralysis. In animal and human nature, the behavioural responses can be fight or flight or even pretending to be dead. Some of these fixed emotional states can sabotage human relationships, cause harm to ourselves and others, and can lead to mental, emotional and physical illness. Often, these emotional responses are deeply ingrained within our physiology, programmed into us at early stages, such as during pregnancy and in the first years of life – before we were able to think or talk.

Transforming negative emotions – such as anxiety, fear, shame and anger – into complex feelings – such as peacefulness, appreciation, enthusiasm, courage, compassion and love – is at the heart of developing a strong will to manifest goals that are in harmonic alignment with the needs of others (harmonic goals). Recognizing and naming negative emotions triggered by adversity, choosing how you want to respond to them constructively, can shift the emotional landscape towards developing positive feelings related to these events. This prepares us for strong, life-transforming actions. The Quick Stress Relief technique below utilizes the coherence breathing process of the Mastery of Life meditation, as this can deepen the transformation into a permanent change within our physiology.

Quick Stress Relief

The following exercise combines paced breathing to balance the autonomic nervous system with a cognitive behavioural therapy technique. Combining the physiological and psychological exercises will allow you not only to reduce the negative impact of pressure on health, judgement and decision-making, but also to process the issues or events that have led to the experience of negative stress and extreme emotions. The exercise aids in neutralizing the latter and helps create a sense of empowerment. It also offers instant, day-to-day stress-relief.

Summary of benefits:
- Relieves stress and extreme emotions.
- Helps in processing challenging situations.
- Prepares for good judgement and decision-making under pressure.
- Enhances performance and productivity under pressure.

Step 1: Breathe Slowly and Deeply (for two minutes)
- Practise coherence breathing as described in Chapter 2 (Mastery of Life meditation).

Step 2: Recognize Your Emotions (30–90 seconds)
- What makes you feel upset?

- How does it make you feel?
- Name your emotion/s as precisely as possible.
- Where in your body do you feel uncomfortable and how?
- Why do you feel that way?

Step 3: Choose Your Emotional and Behavioural Response (30–90 seconds)

- How will you respond now and in similar situations in the future?
- How will I feel?
- What will I do about it?
- Imagine for a moment how it will look and feel when you have implemented your intended response with confidence (mental rehearsing).

In summary:

- Breathe slowly and deeply throughout.
- Choose an upsetting event in the past, present or future.
- Ask yourself how it makes you feel and name your emotion/s.
- *Where* in your body do you feel that emotion and *how* does it feel?
- Now ask yourself why you feel that way?
- Next, ask yourself how you would like to feel and behave, now and in similar situations in the future.
- Mentally rehearse these new emotional responses and behaviours with confidence (mental rehearsing).

8.
Active Listening

Summary: This chapter introduces a technique that helps improve and deepen human relationships, enhancing our perceptiveness to the needs of others.

Context: On the path towards embracing the needs of others and building new communities rooted in selfless love, we require listening skills that are built on being open-minded, open-hearted and open-willed. The qualities of empathy, compassion and love can be acquired through practising active listening whilst suspending judgement, and having unconditional regard to the other person.

Suspending judgement with unconditional regard

Establishing excellent relationships requires the capacity to listen sincerely and to understand – to genuinely appreciate and communicate well. As you suspend your judgement and deepen your interest whilst listening to the other person, you will deepen rapport, understanding and improve your relationships. When suspending judgement, you can open yourself to the object of your observation. This allows perceived impressions to resonate within you, creating thoughts, feelings and images that rise up as an inner response. The insights achieved through this mode of perception will be deeper, more intuitive and therefore more in tune with the object of observation.

Extending your perception and undivided attention in order to develop an intuitive understanding of your surroundings – both human and non-human – will considerably reduce stress, enhancing your health and your vitality. It can also create a deep sense of joy and connectedness to life. Acknowledging how strongly our encounter of the world is affected by (conscious and subconscious) judgements and biases – that often have developed as result of past experiences – is the first step of this process of overcoming them.

Anybody who attempts to listen to somebody who for example has a different world-view or political opinion, knows how difficult it is to silence one's inner judge. In fact, when starting to practise this exercise, one requires considerable energy to actively suppress any surfacing judgements and to enter into a process of pure and active listening.

This process of active listening allows the thoughts, feelings and intentions of the other person into our consciousness without being interrupted by our own thoughts, feelings and intentions. An act of willful selflessness is required for moments of listening; the capacity to let go of one's own thoughts, feelings and intentions in order to become one with the consciousness of the other person – to 'walk in their shoes' and to see the world through the eyes of another. Any honest and truthful effort on this path trains our capacity to love and to develop intuition.

The activity that is asked for here is one of encountering the other person in a childlike way, full of burning interest and awe. What would it mean for our relationships if we could maintain this deep sense of interest, curiosity and devotion – even towards those people we have known for a long time? In effect, we are trying to experience encounters with our partners, relatives and friends as if we have met them for the first time.

There are three steps or levels in this process:

1. The first step is being *'open-minded'*, by actively suspending judgement.
2. The second step is being *'open-hearted'*, allowing the warmth of compassion, gratitude, and love to enter the relationship.
3. The third step is being *'open-willed'*, allowing us to perceive the developmental needs of the other person, and how we can contribute towards furthering these.

Active listening, with an open mind, open heart and open will is truly transformative for both the listener and the person who is perceived and received in that way. It is one of the essential elements of any deeper therapeutic processes, and can also be described as 'empathy'. Our inner strength and goodness develop as we put the deeper needs of the other person above our own and act accordingly.

Otto Scharmer refers to the above three 'open' qualities when he describes that we need to transcend our 'ego-system' in order to find solutions to the most burning questions of our time. Carl Rogers – a humanistic psychotherapist – and his pupils identified this process as the core element of any therapeutic transformation. Rogers asserts that empathy helps clients:

- To pay attention and value their experiencing.
- To see earlier experiences in new ways.
- To modify their perceptions of themselves, others and the world.

- To increase their confidence in making choices and pursuing a course of action.*

In 2002, Jeanne Watson stated that 60 years' of research had consistently demonstrated that empathy is the most powerful determinant of client progress in therapy. She put it this way:

> Therapists need to be able to be responsively attuned to their clients and to understand them emotionally as well as cognitively. When empathy is operating on all three levels – interpersonal, cognitive and affective – it is one of the most powerful tools therapists have at their disposal.†

As we will see, the active listening process that we have described here involves listening not only for the content that is being expressed, but also perceives the emotions, feelings and intentions, as well as authenticity and the alignment of thinking, feeling and will of the other person. This is initially not an act of interpretation, but an act of pure, intentional perception. And it includes not just the understanding of concepts, but also the perceptions of non-verbal elements, such as pitch, volume and flow of voice, posture, gesture and facial expression.

Every conversation should live in the dual 'rhythmic' process of:

- Intense and pure listening, where we attempt to become one with the other person.

---

* Rogers, C. R. (1959). *A Theory of Therapy, Personality, and Interpersonal Relationships: As Developed in the Client-Centered Framework.*

† Watson, J. C. (2002). *Re-visioning Empathy.* Quoted in D. J. Cain (Ed.), *Humanistic Psychotherapies: Handbook of Research and Practice* (pp. 445-471). American Psychological Association, Washington, DC.

- Being completely 'within ourselves' in processing and making sense of what is expressed and received.

That's why we shouldn't abolish judgement, but rather suspend it. Instead of multitasking and processing information whilst receiving it, we separate these processes and intentionally practise one activity at a time. In usual conversations, we may listen whilst at the same time remember past experiences, analysing what it all means for us and working out how we can utilize this new information in future. But nobody is good at multitasking, and in fact our mind is actually switching constantly from one activity to the other. If this switching is not slowed down considerably, then none of these activities is performed particularly well. Imagine you had to listen to a talk and answer an email simultaneously. How would this influence the quality of both activities?

Giving our *undivided attention* to listening before we actually process the information received, gives strength and depth to each of these activities. You will intuit the other person profoundly, creating a much deeper connection, insight and rapport. This potentially transforms our human encounters into therapeutic processes and acts of love.

Summary of the steps:

- Deepen and slow down your breathing and focus on being calm and appreciative.
- Focus on the other person: their voice, pitch and rhythm of speech, breathing, expression and gestures.
- Focus not just on what is being said, but also on *how* it is said.

- Avoid and supress any immediate judgement or emotional response.
- After having carefully listened in the mode of suspended judgement, focus for a short while on your thoughts and feelings about the person.
- Recognize the other person's feelings, needs and intentions.
- Whilst responding, refocus on the person.

The duration of listening with undivided attention may vary depending on the situation and one's current level of skill (thirty seconds up to five minutes). Give yourself time to let the experience reverberate within you and to form your judgements after you have listened with undivided attention. In practice, you can of course select the conversations that are suitable for active listening.

In my years of experience as a GP and clinical specialist, I have experienced repeatedly how powerfully transformative this active listening can be – for myself and the person I am actively listening to – never mind the original purpose of the consultation! It builds the necessary trust, rapport and transformative relationships to facilitate the development of confidence and the motivation to make positive and meaningful changes. And, whenever I practise this exercise, I also experience its positive effect within my own personal relationships.

9.
Mindful Nature Meditation

Summary: Here we introduce a mental exercise that improves and deepens our relationship with the natural world through intuitive insight, loving feelings and firm intentions, with the purpose of creating a new unity on a spiritual level.

Context: Mindful nature observation can powerfully enhance our ability to concentrate and create strong imaginations, which are required when visualizing the symbols of our Mastery of Life meditation and when visualizing goal achievement. Observing natural objects – such as plants, clouds or the blue sky – with undivided attention and the exclusion of any thought processes, letting those impressions reverberate within ourselves, creates not only a stronger memory but also enhances our capacity to *imagine* with strong feelings and intentions. This aids the process of goal achievement, which is based on an enhancement of the powers of imagination and will.

Benefits:
- Enhances your emotional and physical health and wellbeing;
- improves focus and concentration;
- trains one to suspend judgement;
- enhances depth of perception;
- connects with the spirit of nature on a deeper level;
- develops intuitive insight and understanding;
- strengthens imagination;
- enhances focus on living in *the now* or present.

For many people, the relationship with nature has been negatively impacted by the advancement and increased use of technology. More time is spent indoors and in front of screens – such as mobile phones, tablets, laptops, computers and televisions – and less time within human relationships or nature. For many children, human interactions have been largely replaced by screen time.

Social deprivation, nature deprivation – or 'nature deficit disorder' – may have a profound impact on our mental and emotional health. Spending more quality time in nature, doing activities such as gardening, walking or observing, seems to have a very beneficial effect on stress reduction and the improvement of mental and physical health.

With the help of the exercise below, you will be able to enter fully into a state of perception with undivided attention, thus leading to an extension and deepening of what you see and your intuitive insight. By suspending judgement, you can open yourself fully to the object of your observation. This allows perceived impressions to resonate deep within you, creating thoughts, feelings and images that will rise up as an inner response. The insights achieved through this mode of perception, and its reverberation within our mind, are usually more profound, more intuitive and therefore more in tune with the object of observation. Goethe's scientific nature research is based on this methodology, also known as 'Goethean observation'.

In his book *Knowledge of the Higher Worlds, How is it Achieved?*, Rudolf Steiner describes how the application of the mindful and meditative approach towards nature can open the perception and understanding of the world of spirits that live within it. This could also be described as a supersensitive perception of nature, for example of minerals, plants, animals and humans – and even so-called elemental beings (or nature spirits). Such experiencing can help us live in greater harmony with the world.

Steps to extending sensory perception

The following exercise guides us towards the process of mindful observation:

- Slow down and deepen your breathing.
- Focus entirely on a natural object (for example, a plant, an animal, the sky or the ocean), absorbing all details and engaging all your senses (sight, sound, smell, taste, warmth, touch, movement and balance).
- For the moment avoid any judgement or reflection.
- Focus on sensory perceptions rather than on thoughts or inner images that may arise within you.
- If thoughts and images arise, suppress them and refocus on perceiving.
- Take a warm and deep interest in all the details of your observation.
- After a few minutes of undivided attention, focus on your inner response, becoming aware of the feelings, thoughts and images that have been generated within you.

This exercise offers a means to go beyond narrow, self-focused experience.

10.
Developing the Third Eye, Etheric Heart and Etheric Forebone

Summary: The pineal and pituitary glands and the heart are physical organs that correlate to psycho-spiritual processes in consciousness. All organs are in a process of constant evolution. By developing the psycho-spiritual function of these organs and gaining conscious control over them through meditative practice, spiritual consciousness can be extended (clairvoyance, initiation) and imagination and willpower can be enhanced. This results in the development of inner freedom and love, mastery of life and more effective goal realization.

Life is not only a function of material processes, but also the creator of matter. The primordial life force penetrates all existence in the cosmos. As much as physical existence in the world is confined to its objects, the universal life force creates a network in which every part relates to the other. It's like a universal network of forces that penetrates every animated being and manifests physically, in the dimension of time, as development. There have been many names for this universal life force, such as tao, prana, chi, orgon and vril.

In our current phase of human development, human consciousness has learned to master the forces of the physical world – such as electricity, magnetism, nuclear energy, gravity – through science and technology (physics, chemistry, biology), sociology, art and political life.

The next human evolutionary process is to regain mastery over the universal life force consciously. This process starts with self-mastery of the creative life forces within

us, and then extends towards the mastery of the universal life forces in nature. Meditative practice, martial arts,
yoga practice and eurythmy, for example, all work towards
this mastery over the universal life force. Some of these
techniques do it in a traditional, sometimes atavistic, way
whilst other methods are more suitable for contemporary
Western consciousness.

In his prophetic science fiction novel, *Vril, The Coming
Race*, Sir Edward Bulwer-Lytton describes a future society
in which everyone has developed mastery over vril, the
universal life force. It describes a future society that will
be built on free ethics and mutual respect and love. In
his lecture 'The Temple Legend, The Royal Art in a New
Form', Rudolf Steiner indicates, just like Bulwer-Lytton,
that mastery of life will not only enhance our spiritual,
moral and personal development, but will also contribute
towards the building of new societies inspired by selfless
love. Although humanity as a whole will reach this state of
development in the future, some individuals can prepare
and anticipate this process through meditative, ritual and
magical practice. Closely connected with mastery of life is
the spiritual development of the heart and the third eye
(pituitary and pineal gland).

The Mastery of Life meditation serves as a tool to accelerate and enhance this development of skills that one day
will be enjoyed by the whole of humanity. It does it by
meditatively projecting the symbol of the Tau cross into
the third eye and heart, whilst simultaneously sounding a
mantra which stands in close connection with the development of Christ consciousness.

We will now consider the three etheric (life) organs that
are important for the Mastery of Life meditation: the third
eye, the etheric heart and the etheric forebone.

Spiritual development of the third eye (crown and brow chakra)

Chakras (from Sanskrit, meaning wheel, discus, circle), are organs of the astral body (see below) – respectively, soul organs which serve the perception and mastery of the soul world. They are also called lotus flowers, derived from the sacred Indian Lotus, because they appear to the clairvoyant as circular, flower-like forms. In modern human beings, they stand still but can be set in motion through spiritual training. (Modern clairvoyance is associated with strict control of thought.) In the advanced clairvoyant, they rotate clockwise and thus open him or her to a view of the spiritual world. There are seven main chakras.

The third eye, which comprises the harmonically developed brow and crown chakras, is a spiritual organ that lies in the centre of the head, behind the point between the eyebrows and above. It is part of our spiritual makeup called the astral body, the carrier of consciousness, which is responsible for our thinking, feeling and will, and is also the carrier of our raw emotions. Over time, we transform these emotions, such as anxiety, anger, shame and fear, into higher feelings, such as gratitude, appreciation, love and enthusiasm. Through this transformation we begin to organize our astral body.

Once the astral body is organized to some degree, we start to transform our etheric body (or life body), which is done by mastering our more enduring habits and temperaments. The process of organizing and transforming our etheric body is a much slower one. Over time, however, this helps us to master life processes within us and in nature. This transformative work and organization of our astral and etheric bodies is done by our human I, the 'I am'.

When the third eye (brow and crown chakra) and the heart chakra are harmoniously developed, opened and mastered, they allow for certain forms of clairvoyant spiritual perceptions through 'Imagination' (via the brow chakra), 'Inspiration' (via the heart) and 'Intuition', for spiritual creation within the etheric (life) and physical worlds – effectively manifesting harmonic goals, ideas and ideals into reality. The development of the brow chakra also helps to manifest the experience of the 'I am', our higher self – the Christ – within our thinking.

The third eye develops through bringing willfulness, focus and dynamism into our thinking, and by freeing this thinking from the influence of sensory experience through meditation and contemplation. This can be done, for example, through studying spiritual science and by thinking that is free of sensory perception (i.e., in philosophical, mathematical and spiritual concepts).*

The opening and use of the brow chakra facilitates our capacity to experience the spiritual world in the form of Imaginations. It also allows us to shape pictures of our own future that we seek to create, and therefore contributes in a major way to the process of magic, which is based on combining strong imagination with strong feelings and willpower. The development of the brow chakra also prepares for the development and mastery of the crown chakra, which lies above the brow chakra. (The brow chakra lies close to the pituitary gland and the crown chakra lies close to the pineal gland.)

The crown chakra connects us with the universal life forces within our thinking, allowing us to perceive and

* A safe path of training for the development of the brow and crown chakra, for a scientifically educated modern consciousness, is outlined in Rudolf Steiner's book *The Philosophy of Freedom*, which is also in effect a training manual for thinking that is free of sensory perception.

handle the archetypes (pure spiritual ideas) that create our existence. These are then converted into Imaginations and, through the etheric heart and etheric forebone, are transformed into physical reality. The development of brow and crown chakras can also be supported through meditative focus on the third eye, the region within our head (centre, on the level of our eyes), using a mantra and/or spiritual symbol.

In our meditation, the crossing of the three arms of the Tao cross is projected into the region of the pituitary gland, whilst the Sun on top of the cross embraces the pineal gland. For a healthy evolution of our supersensible bodies, it is important to develop the brow chakra and heart chakras together, so that the forces of the head (thinking) and heart (feeling) can unite harmonically.

Spiritual development of the heart chakra and the etheric heart

The heart chakra, which is closely connected to our physical heart, is an organ of empathy, compassion and love. It is the centre of our sevenfold chakra system. It develops through the harmonizing and aligning of thinking, feeling and will. It matures through the development of six distinct qualities: clear thinking, strength of will, equanimity, positive thinking and feeling, the ability to suspend judgement and, finally, the balance of all these five qualities.*

To work on these qualities, and to make them into habits and personality traits, is of great importance as they protect

---

* Rudolf Steiner introduced six 'subsidiary exercises' as a training path to develop this important chakra, as described in his book *Occult Science* in the chapter 'About Initiation'. These exercises are also well described in the book *Enlivening the Chakra of the Heart* by Florin Lowndes.

us from negative influences that can arise from meditative and magical practices, and helps us to develop a balance of thinking, feeling and will – a balance that is a foundation for advancement on the path of inner freedom and selfless love. Thus, this work (described in Chapter 4) should be a priority, as it prepares the path for safe meditative and magical practice.

As these six qualities become habitual, a new centre is built within the etheric organization, connected with the etheric heart. The activity of the heart chakra, which is formed and activated in the astral body through meditation, imprints itself into the etheric body and thus gradually forms the etheric heart centre. A fifth etheric chamber will be built in the heart through these qualities and through our connection with Christ. This will allow us to master the life forces within and around us. The functioning of the heart will then not only be involuntary, but will also be influenced by the human will, in order to master our feelings and emotions.

The etheric forebone

Occasionally referred to as the 'elementary bone' by Rudolf Steiner, the etheric forebone is an organ of the etheric body. In future, it will be formed at the front of the human being, as a counterpart and complement to the backbone (spinal column), with which it will later combine to form a closed system. It represents a kind of second, purely etheric, spinal column. Through spiritual training – if done in the right way – this development can already be anticipated.

The etheric forebone, which descends in front of our body from the head, is organized by the joint activity of the pineal and pituitary glands. The activity of the crown and brow chakras, which are formed and activated in the astral body through meditation, imprint their activity into the etheric body, and thus gradually form the forebone, lying behind the breastbone. The etheric forebone, third eye and etheric heart centre are important tools to master life (prana, vril) within and around us.

The etheric forebone evolves because of the flowing life forces that originate from the transformation of blood into ether (life) within the heart. This stream of life that stems from the etherization of the blood within the heart, flows from the heart into the pituitary gland. It meets the cosmic etheric forces, that stream from the pineal gland into the heart. Both streams meet in the brain and heart and contribute towards the creation of the third eye.*

Our meditation supports the development of the brow, crown and heart chakras within the astral body and the etheric third eye, etheric heart centre and etheric forebone. This development needs to be supported by moral development, and especially by the development of the aforementioned six soul qualities and habits. If moral development is insufficient, the elementary backbone and the crown, brow and heart chakras will develop poorly, easily becoming a point of attack for adversary powers.

Coherence breathing

As we have seen, the meditation of symbols and mantras is further supported by coherence breathing. Breathing with the whole chest, at a pace of five to six cycles per minute (breathing five to six seconds in and five to six seconds out) aligns the – electromagnetic – activity of brain and

---

* See Rudolf Steiner's *The Etherization of Blood*.

heart. Furthermore, a resonance is created between breathing rhythm, blood pressure rhythm and our heart rate's variability, as we breathe with the same pace with which our blood pressure naturally goes up and down (which is approximately six times per minute, or every ten seconds).

As a result of this resonance, heart rate variability – a measure for the rhythmic balance, flexibility and adaptability of our body systems – is profoundly increased. Heart rate variability is a measure for health, optimal emotional regulation and sustainable peak performance. It is increased during positive engagement (doing things with confidence, joy, enthusiasm or love) or generally when one experiences positive states of feeling. Heart rate variability is reduced when one experiences raw, 'negative' emotions, such as anxiety, fear, anger, shame and sadness.

During the coherence breathing process, all body rhythms are enhanced, and one's body and mind enter into a state of focused relaxation. This balanced and highly flexible state of physiology helps us access a meditative state that allows for a full alignment of the physiology and consciousness of our brain (cognition) and heart (higher feelings).

Focusing on the symbols and mantras during the practise of brain/heart coherence through resonant breathing, allows us to better access the transformative power of symbols and mantras, and trains our organism to access a sustainable peak performance state (engagement). Utilizing coherence breathing in our meditative practice aligns the activity of brain and heart and allows us to overcome the resistance within our physical body to opening to the forces living in symbols, mantras and within our aligned goals.

11.
An Initiatory Story: The Temple Legend

Below is an initiatory story written – according to Rudolf Steiner – by the leading Master of Western and Esoteric Christianity, Christian Rozenkreuz. The Temple Legend of Hiram and Solomon depicts Christian Rosenkreuz's initiation during his previous earthly incarnation as Hiram Abiff. However, it also offers a vision for the future development of the individual and humanity. In this regard, the story represents content for personal contemplation and meditation, and complements the meditations we have introduced above.

Working with the story releases forces within our consciousness that lead to transformation and initiation into the world of spirit, connecting us with Christ and Christian Rosenkreuz, both of whom can assist us on our spiritual and earthly path towards initiation and the practice of white magic. The Temple Legend also holds a key for the understanding of the symbol of the Tau cross and our master mantra, which is at the heart of our meditation practice. The mastery of life through meditation on the Tau cross and the master mantra, and the resulting transformation of the inner forces – residing within our nervous system and heart – is depicted in the Temple Legend, which can also serve as an enhancement of the Mastery of Life meditation.

The famous psychiatrist C. G. Jung believed that mental and vital energy are created through the conflict of opposites. In Jung's view, the alchemical attempt to transmute base metals into gold and silver (with the help of 'the philosopher's stone') was a psychological process.

The symbols used by the alchemists were representative
of what he termed the process of individuation: personal
growth, full integration and mastering of conflicting
functions within our conscious, subconscious and unconscious mind.

One must bring the opposites into balance and complete
union, in order to gain emotional and physical health and
to succeed in the integration of the conscious, subconscious
and unconscious mind – after which process we see the
emergence of one's true self!

In alchemy, this union is known as the *conjunctio*, the
'Royal Wedding'. It represents the union of opposites and,
more specifically, the union of the Queen (of Sheba) and
King (Hiram) – *anima* and *animus*, fire and water, or our
inner male and female aspects. It is the unifying of our
higher self, our human spirit (Hiram) with the purified
human soul (the Queen of Sheba), but also the unifying
of the spirit of nature (Hiram) with human consciousness
(the Queen of Sheba). As a result, one's inner and outer life
become integrated and balanced, and one can enter into a
state of peace, tranquillity, wisdom, love, empowerment,
youthfulness and health.

In this process, the lower, unredeemed part of our
human nature must go through destruction (illness, crisis)
and metaphysical death and be resurrected (reborn) as the
higher self and purified soul, as we develop new faculties that can serve ourselves, our loved ones, society and
humanity. This process is experienced as purification and
empowerment and takes place, as we will see, in the 'fire
of the molten sea'.

The Seal of Solomon, the six-pointed star, represents
the three kingdoms of nature – mineral, plant and animal
– within our organization (the upward pointing triangle),

penetrated harmonically by the three higher, spiritual principles of human existence – our purified and enlightened thinking (wisdom), purified and inspired feeling (love) and purified and intuiting will (power). In external culture they represent science, art and state building (or politics).

These higher attributes of human nature are represented in the golden triangle that Hiram receives from his ancestor Cain. Hiram also receives the hammer or Tau cross from Cain, which is the symbol for mastery of the forces of life. It is the same symbol that Hiram writes into the air in order to bring together all craftsman who are involved in the building of the temple, the new community built with free will and selfless love.

The final work that Hiram completes with the help of the hammer, the brazen sea, is initially spoiled by 'the three traitors', symbolizing fear, hatred and doubt. But the hammer (tau) gives mastery over us and over life itself. The master work, the creation of the brazen sea, is the symbolic harmony of the elements of fire (power) and water (wisdom), also symbolized in the two triangles in the hexagram. The fruit of this harmony is the development of freedom, selfless love and the harmony of life.

*The Temple Legend**

Just as a plant raises itself above the earth to receive the inspirations of the sun, Solomon raised his mind to receive all the wondrous measurements and proportions of points,

---

* As paraphrased by Rudolf Steiner in *The Temple Legend* and re-narrated by Patrick Dixon. Steiner's source was Charles William Heckelthorn, *The Secret Societies of All Ages and Countries*, Vol. I, Book VIII, Chapter 1 (1875). This version of the tale has been further edited for publication here.

lines, planes and angles of what would become the great temple – the temple his father didn't have time to build. He opened his heart until it was ready to make concrete the ideal conceived in the heights, so that it might be deeply founded on earth. To make the ideal a reality, he would need the help of a master builder and mason, also supremely skilled in metallurgy, carpentry and glasswork; an artisan who developed, as perfectly as humanly possible, all the crafts and arts that had been handed down from his ancestors, to reach the most complete expression. This was Hiram Abif.

On the other side, King Solomon could be seen as one who had ascended the peaks of wisdom, from where he could survey all the wonders of the word in the world, and the worlds in the word – a poet, peacemaker and philosopher-king. These two, working together, were as the uniting of two streams that in ancient times had diverged from a single source, and ever since run parallel to each other, but now could be reconciled in a single project – as two dreams that sought to wake to one reality – the temple.

At their first meeting, Solomon spoke saying: 'Hiram, I know you are the only one capable of realizing, in outer form, the vision I have received.' Hiram answered: 'I feel honoured, and shall aim to prove that your choosing of me was wise. I feel that my destiny and all I have learnt has led me to this task. The temple will be the realization, fulfilment and triumphant climax of all that my hands can shape.'

So, Hiram, with teams of workers, set about building the temple. And Solomon, while this was going on, continued as a light of wisdom to his subjects, dispensing wise judgements in all the affairs of state – his thoughts and words bringing healing and harmony amidst all the problems of his people's daily lives.

As the temple neared completion, news of its construction – and the great wisdom of Solomon that had made it possible – had spread far and wide beyond his kingdom and reached the attention of the Queen of Sheba, the legendary ruler of a country south of Egypt, on the Nile. So moved was the queen by tales of Solomon's wisdom and the great temple, that she decided to take a long journey so that she might question him and hear his answers, and look upon the marvel of the temple.

After a long and arduous journey, her great caravan, consisting of many servants, camels, horses and mules laden with gifts of gems, rare fabrics, embroidered silks and aromatic spices, arrived in Solomon's kingdom. He had been informed of her coming and prepared a welcoming ceremony and festivity that spared no expense. Upon first seeing her, he exclaimed: 'Your beauty surpasses all the descriptions I have heard.'

In the next days, she spent most of her time with Solomon, walking in the palace gardens, listening to his words as he answered her many questions. She said to him: 'In your words, it is as if I hear super-earthly music that lifts my mind into harmonies of boundless wonder.' Solomon felt as if he was falling – as sunlight falls upon a beautiful flower that it seeks to open; as a sun that wants to pour all its light into one flower and bathe in her colours and perfumes – forgetting that he must also shine equally for all his people.

On impulse he said: 'Marry me. Together we can do so much more, be so much more, than we can be apart; between your beauty and my truth, through our love, we can bring to birth a greater goodness than will ever walk upon the earth.'

The Queen of Sheba knew there was truth in what he said and replied: 'Yes, I will become your wife, and will pledge myself to you with this ring.' So, for the moment all was well with the world.

Then the queen asked Solomon if she could see the temple. Solomon, proud of his achievement, agreed and the queen was taken to it, just as the finishing touches were being applied. She was filled with wonder at the astonishing artistry, and marvelled at the skill and industry that had gone into it. The outside of the temple awakened the beholder to the mysteries of inner being, whilst on entering, all the forms, arches, columns and vaults led the eye to a sense of infinite space, which spoke of that which was beyond time.

She turned to Solomon and said: 'I would love to meet the one whose hands and work fashioned all these earthly elements into such a heavenly structure.'

It was like the beginning of an eclipse; a shadow crossed the light of Solomon's mind. He could not really explain it, but he did not want her to meet Hiram. He resisted her request, but eventually relented. From his high place of wisdom, Solomon had fallen in love. Now he was falling a second time, into the pit of possessiveness and jealousy – forgetting that one can be possessed by love, but not possess the thing that one loves, but rather, to set it free.

The Queen of Sheba met Hiram. He looked up from his work, looked at her face, then he looked into her eyes, and the light of his eyes illuminated something in her heart, like a treasure hidden deep in the earth. Solomon had lifted her mind, with his words, into wide vistas of seeing; Hiram stirred her depths, with the look of an artist seeing her inner beauty that lived within the temple of her outer form.

Under Hiram's gaze, the queen felt all the elements of her being melting in the flame that was beginning to glow in the fire that was kindled in her heart; not just a flower opening to light, but a root that was grounding itself in all the mysteries of Mother Earth – growing out of it as a daughter of the elements, to combine as the purest expression of the primal enigma of woman.

For a moment, she could not speak; then she said to Solomon, as if to deflect the awareness of what was irresistibly growing inside her: 'Can I meet all the workers who helped to build the temple?' Solomon, who now felt her slipping away from him, said: 'There are too many of them; it would not be possible to gather them all from their tasks so quickly. I think we should return to the gardens.'

At this, Hiram, in order to be better seen, leapt upon a stone and motioned in the air with his right hand the symbolical tau. Immediately, men hastened from all parts of the work and into the presence of their master. This impressed the queen more deeply, and she began to regret her promise of marriage to the king, as she now felt a love for Hiram that came from the very centre of the world.

Solomon now felt himself to be in darkness and sensed a growing darkness within him. All his lofty wisdom seemed empty and vain if he could not hold the love of this woman. What did Hiram have that he did not? He was a great king, renowned for his inspired wisdom, for all his riches and his famous gardens.

Now, Solomon the wise began to fall from the heights into that which was base and unwise; he plotted to destroy Hiram and the love growing between him and the queen. How could he discredit him? He heard that there were three of Hiram's workers who bore a grudge against him, as he had refused to confer upon them the status of master craftsmen. He had claimed they had neither knowledge, and neither did they apply themselves enough to the work to earn the status of master. One was a Syrian mason, another a Phoenician carpenter and a third a Hebrew miner.

This triangle of darkness now formed within Solomon a conspiracy, a confederacy of jealousy, and Solomon – who had conceived the temple of *wisdom* in the service of *love*, was now engaged in that which would bring about the destruction of *truth*, and the destruction of that which would bring about the creation of *love*.

The three craftsmen now became three crafty and cunning agents of those invisible powers that would always oppose everything for which the temple was built. One said: 'I always thought I deserved to be a master; I will make him think again about denying me.' Another said: 'I feel deeply slighted; may he know the feeling of humiliation I felt.' And the third said: 'He has done us a great wrong, and it is right that we should do unto him what he did to us.'

Now, that which was to be the crowning achievement of Hiram's work was the molten sea, cast in bronze, which was to have adorned the temple. All the necessary mixtures of ores had been prepared in a most wonderful manner. The molten sea was to mirror the molten sea of love that was rising in the heart of the queen, from all the disparate elements of her being.

However, the conspiring workers adulterated the metals of the casting, and added substances that would cause a catastrophic failure – just as distrust and jealousy can cause all relationships to end in failure and disaster. For the molten sea was to be an expression of a new union and cooperation of hitherto separated elements, to bring about a never-to-be-experienced-before harmony between the inestimable heights and the unfathomable depths of the world.

A young workman discovered the plot to sabotage Hiram's work, and he revealed it to Solomon, thinking that Solomon would act against the plotters – but Solomon did nothing to prevent it, as his secret jealousy caused him to wish for Hiram's destruction.

The day of the casting arrived, and the Queen of Sheba was present. At the critical moment, however, the whole casting failed. A crack, as of thunder, rent the air, as if the underworld was to erupt and overflow over all of nature. It was just as the plotters had hoped, yet they also feared what the darkness within them had invoked in outer nature. The doors that had restrained all the molten metal were forced open, and torrents of liquid fire poured into the vast mould where the brazen sea was to assume its form. But the burning mass overflowed the edges of the mould, endangering all who had come to view the casting, and they fled from the advancing river of fire.

Calmly and coolly, Hiram tried to arrest the lava-like flow, dousing it with copious amounts of water. The water and the fire mixed in a primal elemental battle; the water rose as a dense steam and fell as a boiling rain, spreading panic among the crowd. Feeling ashamed by this catastrophe, Hiram sought the sympathy of a faithful heart in his friend, but Benoni – who had informed Solomon of the plot – had died trying to avert the catastrophe.

Hiram withdrew, oppressed with grief. He had not heeded the danger and the possibility that this ocean of fire might have speedily engulfed him. He thought of the Queen of Sheba, who had come to admire and congratulate him on his great triumph, and who had now seen nothing but a terrible disaster. Suddenly, in his loneliness he heard a strange voice coming somewhere from above his highest aspirations, and at the same time proceeding from a depth that was deeper than his most profound knowledge.

It cried: 'Hiram! Hiram!' He looked up and beheld a gigantic figure. The apparition continued: 'Come, my son, be without fear, the fire will not harm you; cast yourself into the flames.' Hiram threw himself into the fires – and where others would have found death, he tasted ineffable delights.

He could not withdraw from this state, as he felt drawn by an irresistible force. He asked who was leading him on this strange journey and where was he being taken. The voice answered: 'Into the centre of the earth, where the will of the world is forged, so that which is heaviest may scale the heights of the boundless expanses of light; where all that is base may be led from infinite weight to eternal light, into the kingdom of great Cain, where the future of human freedom is wrought from the bondage of the fallen elements. There can be tasted the fruits of the Tree of Knowledge and Life.'

'Who, then, am I, and who are you?'

'I am the father of your fathers. I am the son of Lamech. I am Tubal Cain.'

Tubal Cain introduced Hiram to the sanctuary of fire and initiated him into the secrets of casting bronze as well as the mysteries of the original and final fires that will consume all Creation. Hiram was led into the presence of Cain, progenitor of his line of descent. Cain taught Hiram about the suffering he and his descendants had to bear, though that suffering was the furnace that had tempered their unconquerable will. He blessed Hiram: 'Go, my son, the fires of living thought and burning will are with you.'

Before he departed, Tubal Cain gave Hiram the hammer, with which he had achieved great things, and a golden triangle, which he carried with him as a pendant around his neck. Tubal Cain said to Hiram: 'Thanks to this hammer and the help of the fires that live, you will speedily accomplish the work left unfinished through man's stupidity and ill will.'

Hiram did not hesitate to use the wonderful power of the hammer he received. And the golden dawn saw the mass of bronze cast. The artist felt a golden light rise from his heart and into his mind, and the queen exalted in the light that shone from his eyes. The people came running, and their astonishment overflowed at the secret power that had been revealed – that in one night had repaired everything.

Then the queen, accompanied by her maids, journeyed out of Jerusalem, and there she encountered Hiram, alone and in deep thought. The encounter was decisive; they confessed their love for each other. They hesitated no longer, but mutually pledged their vows, and deliberated how the queen could retract the vows she had made to the king. Hiram was to be the first to leave Jerusalem. The queen, impatient to re-join him, was to elude the vigilance of the king. This she accomplished by withdrawing the ring that she had given to him whilst he was overcome with wine.

Later, Solomon hinted to the three craftsmen – whom Hiram had denied the degree of master – that the removal of his rival for the hand of the queen was quite acceptable to him. So, when the architect came into the temple, they assailed him. Before his death, however, he had time to throw the golden triangle – which he wore around his neck, and on which was engraved the word of the master – into a deep well.

Eventually, Hiram was found, and was able to utter a few final words. He said: 'Tubal Cain promised me that I shall have a son who will be father of many descendants, who will people the earth, and bring my work, the building of the temple, to completion.' Then he pointed to the place where the golden triangle was to be found. This was then collected and brought with the hammer to the molten sea, and both were preserved together, in the Holy of Holies.

The triangle was further concealed by a cubical stone, on which had been inscribed the sacred law: 'Only those who can understand the meaning of the legend of the Temple of Solomon and its master builder Hiram, can discover the golden triangle, the hammer and the molten sea.'

12.
The Molten Sea and Communities Based on Love

The molten or brazen sea was, according to the Old Testament account, a round basin cast in bronze by the temple builder Hiram of Tyre (Hiram Abif) for the forecourt of Solomon's temple. The basin rested on a base of twelve bronze oxen. The Bible describes the monumental casting of the basin thus:

> Then he made the molten sea; it was round, ten cubits from brim to brim, and five cubits high, and a line of thirty cubits measured its circumference. Under its brim were gourds, for thirty cubits, compassing the sea round about; the gourds were in two rows, cast with it when it was cast. It stood upon twelve oxen, three facing north, three facing west, three facing south, and three facing east; the sea was set upon them, and all their hinder parts were inward. Its thickness was a handbreadth; and its brim was made like the brim of a cup, like the flower of a lily; it held two thousand baths.*

The casting of the brazen sea forms the core of the Temple Legend. It is a symbol for what needs to be achieved by humanity in the future – and which can already be worked upon by those who lead the way on the ascending developmental path of humanity. It is the harmonic connection between the element of water, representing calm wisdom, and the element of fire, representing passion and power.

---

* 1 Kings 7:23-26. Revised Standard Version (1952).

The Molten Sea (Holman Bible, 1890)

The final work, of casting the brazen sea in the forecourt
of the temple, had been well prepared by Hiram. But Solomon, in his jealousy, instructed three sworn enemies of
Hiram to ruin this final work. These three workmen or
apprentices, to whom Hiram denied the title of a master
because of their incompetence, mixed elements into the
flow of the ore which made the whole work go up in flames.

On a symbolic level, these three evil apprentices represent *doubt* in the truth of wisdom; *superstition*, as false
beliefs about the constitution of the spiritual world; and
the *illusion* of the personal self that makes us experience
ourselves as separate from each other and, in our selfishness, stops us from embracing each other as representing
one humanity.

In his darkest moments of despair, Hiram hears a voice
from the interior of the earth, asking him to throw himself

into the flames. As he throws himself in, he does not experience death, as others would, but rather experiences his initiation into the secrets of working with metals and the development of human consciousness. He travels to the inner earth, where he receives the hammer (the Tau cross), the golden triangle and the master word.

On his return to the temple, with the help of the hammer (tau), he manages to restore the brazen sea, the symbol of harmony through love between wisdom and power.

Building new Communities based on Selfless Love

Hiram and Solomon are representatives of two previously opposing groupings of mankind.

The Solomonic stream represents the receiving of the pure, passionless wisdom as an act of priestly receptiveness. The principle of *belief* is in the foreground: passive and devoted reception of God's gifts, leaving God's creation unchanged.

Solomon was able to conceive all the shapes and measures of the temple, which is the representation of the spiritual nature of our physical body, and a place of worship that allows the revelation of God in the Holy of Holies. Solomon needed Hiram's skills as a master builder to complete his work.

Hiram is of a different genealogy than Solomon. He is *not* a son of passionless wisdom, which is represented through the element of water. Rather, Hiram is the son of passion and wilfulness, represented through the element of *fire*.

Both needed each other to complete the great work of the temple – but they also did not get on with each other. And the fateful, destructive aspect of their relationship was created through the competing love for Balkis, the Queen of Sheba, who initially promises marriage to Solomon, but then ultimately turns her love to Hiram. She experiences that the future development of humanity does not lie in passionless wisdom, but in the powerful creations of the human will.

Hiram's fiery willpower is like the sun, and Solomon's passionless wisdom is like the moon. Balkis, who represents the human soul, also represents the female quality of the moon, but in a renewed form. She is a symbol of the purified soul (water) that wants to unite itself with the fiery will-nature of Hiram. Both qualities – of sun and moon, fire and water, male and female, wisdom and power – need to be balanced and united in order to advance the development of individuals and humanity as a whole. This balance and unity is expressed in both symbols: the Tau cross with Sun and the brazen sea.

Love is the third element. It unites wisdom and power and allows the harmonization and union of what, for millennia, have been in opposition. As we learn to develop sensual love, through devoted relationships to humans and nature, and develop *spiritual* love on the path of freedom, we unite freedom and love within us and harmonize and unite the two streams of Solomon and Hiram within our individual (human) soul. The result of this is the development of selfless love and unanimity of feelings that will be the new, core building element of spiritual communities that further the advancement of the individual and humanity.

Occult brotherhoods, such as the Freemasons, used to create cultural progression and advancement of human consciousness by thinking and imagining future conditions – for example, the French Revolution and the American Constitution – decades before their time. What was thought and imagined in such a brotherly context then created its own reality. Many of these organizations have become decadent and some are now following purely selfish interests of power.

But there may come a time in the future where spiritual organizations can be founded – without secrecy and with transparency – that support the spiritual development of the individual and humanity towards freedom and selfless love. This will only be possible if people take upon themselves to prepare this path by developing such qualities within themselves. These individuals will then not only become co-creators of a new abundance within themselves and within their own destiny, but will also contribute towards other people accessing this abundance. And abundance is not solely defined by what we have, but also by who we *are* – or what we are on the path of *becoming*.

Further Reading

William Walker Atkinson, *The Secret Doctrine of the Rosicrucian*, Weiser Books 2012

Werner Barfod, *IAO and the Eurythmy Meditation*, Mercury Press 2001

Robert Blumenti, *Vril, The Force of the Gods*, iUniverse 2010

D. E. Bowler; L. M. Buyung-Ali; Knight, A. S. Pullin, 'A systematic review of evidence for the added benefits to health of exposure to natural environments', BMC Public Health 2010

Margarete van der Brink, *More Precious than Light. How Dialogue can Transform Relationships and Build Community*, Temple Lodge Publishing 2021

Edward Bulwer-Lytton, *The Power of the Coming Race*, Trapart Books 2020

Danielle van Dijk, *Christ Consciousness, A Path of Inner Development*, Temple Lodge Publishing 2010

Joe Dispenza, *Becoming Supernatural*, Hay House 2019

Peter Gruenewald, *Manifesting your Best Future Self*, Adaptive Resilience 2021

Peter Gruenewald, *The Quiet Heart, Putting Stress in its Place*, Floris Books 2015

Richard Louv, *Last Child in the Woods: Saving our Children from Nature-Deficit Disorder*, Atlantic Books 2013

Florin Lowndes, *Enlivening the Chakra of the Heart*, Rudolf Steiner Press 2000

T. H. Meyer, *Clairvoyance and Consciousness: The Tao Impulse in Evolution*, Temple Lodge Publishing 2012

T. H. Meyer, *The New Cain, The Temple Legend as a Spiritual and Moral Impulse for Evolution and its Completion by Rudolf Steiner*, Temple Lodge Publishing 2017

Peter J. Morris, *The Power of Ankh*, Kinsett Publishing 2015

Marko Pogačnik, *Christ Power and Earth Wisdom, Searching for the Fifth Gospel*, Clairview 2020

Carl R. Rogers, *Person to Person: The Problem of Being Human*, Souvenir Press Ltd 1994

Otto Scharmer, Katrin Kaufer, *Leading from the Emerging Future: From Ego-System to Eco-System Economies*, Berrett-Koehler Publishers 2013

Rudolf Steiner, *Esoteric Christianity and the Mission of Christian Rosenkreuz*, Rudolf Steiner Press 2000

Rudolf Steiner, *The Etherisation of Blood*, Rudolf Steiner Press 1971

Rudolf Steiner, *Knowledge of the Higher Worlds*, Rudolf Steiner Press 2011

Rudolf Steiner, *Occult Science* (see chapter 'About Initiation'), Rudolf Steiner Press 2011

Rudolf Steiner, *Philosophy of Freedom*, Rudolf Steiner Press 2011

Rudolf Steiner, *Freemasonry and Related Occult Movements from the Contents of the Esoteric School*, Rudolf Steiner Press 2013

Nick Thomas, *Freedom through Love, The Search for Meaning in Life*, Temple Lodge Publishing 2014

M. Townsend; R. Weerasuriya, *Beyond Blue to Green: The Benefits of Contact with Nature for Mental Health and Well-being*, Melbourne 2010

J. C. Watson, 'Re-Visioning Empathy', in D. J. Cain (Ed.), *Humanistic Psychotherapies: Handbook of Research and Practice*, American Psychological Association 2002

Supportive material for the Mastery of Life meditation and the contents of this book can be found on Peter's website: www.mastering-life.com